DREAMING
IMPOSSIBLE
DREAMS

DREAMING IMPOSSIBLE DREAMS

Reflections of an Entrepreneur

E.J. Ourso

with Dan Marin

Acadian House
PUBLISHING
Lafayette, Louisiana

Library of Congress Cataloging-in-Publication Data
Ourso, E.J., 1923-
  Dreaming impossible dreams : reflections of an entrepreneur /
E.J. Ourso with Daniel Barbour Marin.
        p. cm.
  Includes bibliographical references and index.
  ISBN 0-925417-42-4 (hardcover) -- ISBN 0-925417-43-2 (softcover)
  1. Ourso, E. J., 1923- 2. Millionaires—United States—Biography.
  3. Businesspeople—United States—Biography. 4. Philanthropists—United
States—Biography. I. Marin, Daniel Barbour, 1937- II. Title.
  HC102.5.O87 A87 2001
  650.1—dc21
                              2001004560

♦ Published by Acadian House Publishing, Lafayette, Louisiana
  (Edited by Trent Angers; interior graphic design and production by
  Jon Russo)

♦ Cover illustration by Janine Collins, Lafayette, Louisiana

♦ Cover design and production by Elizabeth Bell, Lafayette, Louisiana

♦ Printed by Sheridan Books, Fredericksburg, Virginia

Dedicated to the memory of my faithful wife of 53 years,

Marjory B. Ourso, who believed in me and my impossible dreams

when no one else did.

Acknowledgements

In several places in this book, I suggest it is important to realize that none of us goes it alone, that we achieve our goals with the help of dedicated people and with a generous helping of Divine Providence.

Accordingly, I would like to point out that every agent, manager, funeral director, cemeterian, bookkeeper, secretary, and associate with whom I came in contact in nearly half a century of business contributed something that helped make my impossible dreams come true. Brief stories about many of these good people, and the roles they played in the success of our company, can be found in the pages which follow.

I acknowledge, with gratitude, the contributions made by all of them.

– E.J. Ourso

Table of Contents

PREFACE

A Short Course
In Entrepreneurship

I look forward to talking with the young people who come to see me at my house on St. Charles Avenue in New Orleans. Professor Robert Justis of Louisiana State University brings students from his entrepreneurship classes to the house, and I try to teach them something about business.

He introduces me as Doctor E.J. Ourso. He knows I'm a closet professor. I love to teach. Listening to his introduction, I am taken by a desire to tell these students, all at once, everything about how I've done what I've done. Here's how I made it. This is what it cost. Here are the defeats and triumphs I tasted along the way. But how can I tell it all in just a part of one afternoon?

I immediately disabuse the students of the notion that I'm highly educated, with a PhD. I tell them right off that I don't have a college degree, that the war interrupted my education at LSU and I never got to finish. The "Doctor" is an honorary Doctor of Humane Letters, awarded by LSU in 1997.

"Don't be surprised if I don't sound like your professors at the university," I say.

I talk with them in a large room on the first floor, where we set up chairs and a desk, an informally arranged classroom. The students sit in a semicircle of comfortable chairs. I lean forward, eagerly, elbows on my desk. They are waiting for the truth. I think, *Lord help me.*

I begin by telling them I think this class called "Entrepreneurship" should not be thought of as a class in small business management. No, entrepreneurship is not a matter of small business management. From my point of view, an entrepreneur's angle of vision, a class with this title is about the growing of a business, or something anyway that deals with the idea of expansion and growth. That's fundamental. Most entrepreneurs I've known, or known about - like John Folse or Billy Guillot of Donaldsonville, or like Bill Gates of Microsoft - started out small but immediately set about getting bigger and bigger. John Deere, A.P. Giannini, Hewlett and Packard - they all started out small and got big.

As for my wife Margy and me, we started out with a capital investment of $10,000, then began to grow almost immediately. We made our first acquisition after just two years. We made fifty-six acquisitions in forty-eight years. And, believe it or not, we made the first twenty-five with no money.

"No money?" the students ask skeptically. "How can you make acquisitions with no money?"

"Yup. No money," I tell them. "And we sold our business, Security Industrial Insurance, in a deal valued at $180 million."

As I've said, I can't think about entrepreneurship without thinking about growth. The ideas of growth, expansion and improvement preoccupied me from my first day in business.

That's where I start when I'm teaching the students from LSU.

Of course, I point out the benefits of compound interest and explain the process of building gradually and patiently through repetition.

"Choose a business where your clients come back and back and back. The central idea here is repetition. You don't want to be selling a single item and then another and another, but rather you want to be establishing a pattern, an ongoing service relationship. Insurance is the perfect example. Each week, or month, or year the premiums are paid; the surplus builds up and up. It compounds. However, understand that early encounters establish the foundation for long-term relationships," I explain.

My motive in correcting the notion that I'm some sort of highly educated person is not so much modesty as it is an effort to help them realize how fortunate they really are.

"Look, if an uneducated country boy from Donaldsonville can make it, think what someone with your educational advantages might be able to accomplish. I had to read books and educate myself as I went along. You will start out knowing all sorts of things that I had to learn the hard way," I tell them.

It's important that they understand this point: that they will be launching their careers from a very advantageous position.

I want them to leave my house at the end of the day changed in some real way that will make a difference in their lives.

"I want you to do great," I tell them.

I want to inspire and lift them up. I want to instill in each of them a sense of what's possible.

"With your advantages, with your brains, nothing is impossible," I say.

By this I mean they should dream big, impossible dreams, and then set about making them real. How can I make them see this? How can I make them believe it? This is something I've learned from experience, and from some of the books I've read as well.

For me, inspiration came from reading about A.P. Giannini, who started out as a son of poor Italian immigrants and eventually created Bank of America. Talk about being without advantages. I figured if he could do it with banks starting in San Francisco, why couldn't I do it with burial insurance starting in Donaldsonville, Louisiana? This is the kind of reasoning and belief I want to instill.

My first big job, I tell them, was selling chickens door to door in Donaldsonville. Before that I collected newspaper and scrap iron. When I was twenty-one I was in World War II, in the European Theater. And at the war's end, my father's death at age forty-three brought me back to Donaldsonville to run his funeral home business so I could support my mother and younger sister and brother.

This is not the career I'd had in mind when I went to LSU before the war. But The Man Upstairs knew better than I did what I was cut out for, where I could do the most good. My formal education ended in the middle of my fourth year as a journalism and English literature major.

I tell my students – mine for a brief hour and a half or so – to be overperformers. I urge them to overperform in their studies as well as in other aspects of their lives. People are always surprised when ordinary people do extraordinary things. That's what I mean by overperforming. Surprise everyone.

One and a half hours, then we'll sit down together for dinner, and then they'll be on their way back to Baton Rouge. As the clock runs on the wall behind me, I work hard to compress all I've learned about achieving success into this limited time. But there's so much to say. Success is not a simple thing. It comes in many forms.

While I was a student at LSU I never took any courses in economics or management or accounting or finance, no business strategy or entre-preneurship. Where business is concerned, I learned what I learned on my own from experience and reading. After the war I read a book a day for many years. The great thing about books is that they put you in touch with all kinds of experts in all kinds of fields. I'm partial to biographies and history.

My real education has gone on for years; it has never stopped. So, it's quite a challenge trying to squeeze the important things I've learned about achieving success into my limited time with these students.

Oh, I do my best. I overperform as best I can. I tell them how marry-ing Margy was the best decision I ever made, how I got my education and found my acres of diamonds in Donaldsonville. I tell them about the virtue of perseverance, about the importance of productive employ-ees and healthy self-esteem, and about the obligation to do for others. I tell them how we built the company acquisition by acquisition, about the real power of impossible dreaming, and finally about the big part which Divine Providence played in our success. I tell them stories.

At the end of the session I display the contents of my "Entrepreneur's Start-up Kit," which I give each of them before they leave. I take out the little pocket mirror that's included.

"Look in it each morning and say out loud, 'If it is to be, it is up to me,'" I tell them.

I hold up one of my green pens, green for money. They laugh. I hold up my list of recommended books. There are posters for their walls telling them about the virtue of perseverance. I give them books – Napoleon Hill's *Think and Grow Rich*, Russell Conwell's *Acres of Diamonds*, books about thinking out of the box and how to get ideas. I want them to do great. I'm thinking maybe these tangible things they take with them will stimulate further reflection.

But still there's not enough time. I can only give them an outline, the bare bones of what I want to say. There's no time to elaborate and reflect, nor to flesh out the outline and breathe life into the lessons. I can do only so much in the time I have.

So, I thought, *why not write a book? Why not put down on paper what I know, what I would say to these people if I had more than an hour and a half?*

And that's what I've tried to do in the book you are now holding. Following are the reflections of an entrepreneur. I present them to you in the hope that they will make a difference in your life.

– *E.J. Ourso*

DREAMING IMPOSSIBLE DREAMS

CHAPTER 1

The Best Decision
I Ever Made

ONE HOT AFTERNOON IN THE SUMMER OF 1974
I was talking with a Harvard business administration student
who was working for my company on an internship. This bright,
inquisitive young man had remained in the office after working hours
to ask if I would share with him the secrets of my success.

"What is the best business decision you ever made?" he asked.

I leaned back in my chair and thought about it for only a few seconds.

"Marrying Margy," I answered with certainty. "Best decision, period."

The look in his eye said he believed me, though he couldn't understand how this could possibly be. So I offered to explain it, and he leaned forward in his chair to hear my story.

I first saw Margy in the summer of 1940. I had just finished high school and was taking tickets at the Grand Theater in my hometown of Donaldsonville. T. Royal Casso introduced us. T. Royal Casso, a middle-aged businesswoman, owned the restaurant next door to Weill's Department Store, one of several in Louisiana and Mississippi owned by Margy's parents.

T. Royal appeared at the theater one Saturday afternoon with a pretty girl in tow. As she handed me her ticket, she nodded toward the girl, who was a few years younger than me.

"E.J., this is Margy Barbier. Margy, this is E.J. Ourso."

T. Royal winked and went on into the dark. Margy lingered. There, in the theater lobby, in the soft light, she appeared like a spring flower ready to blossom. Her green eyes held me for a moment; she smiled.

She's the most beautiful girl I've ever seen, I told myself. Never changed my mind. Some inner voice told me this was the chance of my life.

T. Royal meant for Margy and me to get acquainted, which we did. Margy lived in White Castle, which is just a few miles from Donaldsonville; she was a sophomore at White Castle High School. During the summers she stayed in Donaldsonville with her aunt and uncle, who managed Weill's Department Store. She helped out in dry goods, stocking, running errands, assisting the customers. Margy had charming ways.

We liked each other right off, I could tell, though she couldn't have been more than fourteen. I was seventeen, finished with high school, and on my way to college, but T. Royal made sure I saw a lot of Margy that summer. And I saw her from time to time on holidays when I came home from LSU, also thanks to T. Royal.

Then we got into the war. But by the time I joined the Army, Margy occupied a very special place in my heart.

I'm a goal-setter. Brother Alton, my high school football coach, called it "focus."

"E.J.'s got focus," he told my mother.

When it came to winning Margy, if I'd have told anyone what I was aiming at, they'd have said, "Ous, you're crazy," and locked me up. Sometimes it's good planning to keep your goals to yourself. Especially if you're trying for something that everybody but you thinks is impossible. Some impossible dream.

The war got in the way of all sorts of dreams. Uncle Sam called up my Reserve Officer Training Corps (ROTC) unit, interrupting my studies at Louisiana State University in journalism and English literature. And during the war there was Margy's engagement to Frank Heard, a dentist from New Orleans, which I learned about from my Army buddy, Floyd Roberts, Margy's first cousin from White Castle. Right after Hitler's collapse, Floyd and I were in the occupation forces in Germany. Talk about obstacles to your dreams. When Floyd told me the bad news, my heart sank, but I said to myself, *Ous, this isn't the first deck stacked against you.* I'd been through the siege of Bastogne with General Patton and survived.

Before I get to how I married Margy despite these obstacles, I'll tell you who I am and where I'm from, so you can picture the circumstances in which I won this prize. E.J. Ourso's the name, from Donaldsonville, Louisiana. I've talked to a lot of students studying for Master of Business Administration degrees at LSU and some up at Harvard. In the 1970s, I went to Harvard for summer seminars with the Young Presidents Organization, the only YPOer who sold burial insurance. That made me stand out, though not always in a favorable light. Still, the dean put me on the speakers' list because he had never known a man who sold burial insurance. The other YPOers were against it; they took exception to my Cajun accent. The Harvard students seemed to like my nickel-a-stop, twenty-stops-to-the-dollar speech. The Dean invited me back, Cajun accent and all, nine years in a row. But I'm still a country boy, still proud to claim Donaldsonville as my hometown.

My business was Security Industrial Insurance Company. We owned funeral homes and sold burial insurance – insurance for the services we provided. Our ads were on TV. A gold key comes on the screen, then the words, "Security Industrial Insurance: the key to peace of mind." A clear, simple message.

All in all we acquired fifty-six companies – funeral homes and insurance companies – the first twenty-five with no money! No money, because in the beginning we had no money. Now I'm retired. In 1996, after nearly half a century, we sold the insurance company and the funeral homes in a deal valued at approximately $180 million.

I got my start in business as a boy, collecting scrap paper and iron and bone for buttons. This was during the Great Depression, which lasted longer in Donaldsonville than in most other places. After that I sold all of my uncle's seven hundred chickens in one summer. My introduction to sales.

I'll never forget my pitch, developed through much trial and error. First, always go 'round to the back door; it's closer to the kitchen. I'd speak through the screen door.

"Ma'am," I'd say, "wouldn't you like this nice, fat spring chicken for your family's supper this evening?"

I wanted to convey a strong picture of that chicken on the table ready to eat. For an extra nickel I'd wring the chicken's neck. For another dime I'd pluck it.

"Yes, E.J.," the ladies would say, "I'll take one or two of those nice spring chickens."

Would they like me to wring the necks? Most would, for the extra nickel.

"And pluck it, too."

"Yes, ma'am."

G rowing up in Donaldsonville, everybody got a nickname or two. Back when I played on Catholic High's football team, I was known as "Rub, Rub Ourso." As our coach, Brother Alton, would explain, I was hobbled by shin splints and I got addicted to analgesic balm rubs.

I was "Rub" on Brother Hugh's basketball team as well. After that, Coach Ed Khoury of the LSU boxing team called me "Hamburger Ourso," and not because I ate a lot of hamburgers.

"Hamburger Ourso," he'd say, as I lay bloody-faced on the canvas, "Get up and knock the sonofabitch out. Get up, Hamburger."

And I'd get up and get knocked down again.

My Army buddies called me "Ous." Rhymes with "goose." Later my competitors in the funeral business called me "No-Cash-Ous." Driven by necessity, we perfected the art of buying other businesses without paying cash at the front end of the deal.

After many years of very hard work, Margy and I moved to a mansion on St. Charles Avenue in New Orleans. Lots of solid African mahogany woodwork, except in the kitchen, where it's cherry wood. Eight bathrooms and twenty telephones. A Jacuzzi in the master bedroom and another out by the pool. The roof is Spanish tile. Beautiful. We put up a sign: "Only in America." Only in America could such an impossible dream come true.

But, I'm still the same E.J. Ourso who was born and reared in Donaldsonville, a town of about eight thousand souls located on the banks of the Mississippi River in south Louisiana. This town had a lot to do with how I grew up and what I did.

"Never forget where you came from," I'd tell the MBA students from LSU and Harvard.

Marrying Margy

Now I'll tell you how I won Margy's hand.

My father's death at the age of 43 in 1946 brought me back from the occupation force in Neuburg, Germany, to the part of the world where Margy all along had been blossoming like a bright flower in springtime. I was a captain in the Motorized Field Artillery of General Patton's 3rd Army. I was anticipating a career as a commissioned officer, having passed the Officer's Candidate School (OCS) entrance tests and interviews. Then, in March, I got word that my Daddy had died of a heart attack.

On the flight from Paris to New York, bad weather forced the plane to land in Sao Miguel in the Azores. I feared I'd miss the funeral. The ride got bumpy. I looked out the window. Lord help us, were we landing in the middle of the cold, green-gray Atlantic Ocean? Then the Azores came into view. After a night in the Sao Miguel airport, the sky cleared, the wind dropped, and we flew on to New York. I was to connect with a plane for Memphis, and from there to fly on to New Orleans. Of course, I missed my connection. The only plane to Memphis until the next day was full except for one seat, and several people were fighting for it.

But luck was with me. General Chennault, who knew me, had a seat on that plane, and when he heard I was trying to get home for my father's funeral, he interceded on my behalf and secured the seat for me. Help from above? Do you think your soul goes it alone? The war showed me it does not.

The funeral cortege went from the mortuary for several blocks to the

Church of the Ascension of Our Lord Jesus Christ. The cemetery is near the church, in sight of the levee, which had already grown green. A warm spring breeze came off the Mississippi River.

Just about the whole town attended. Daddy was a kind and generous man, well liked and respected by his neighbors. His heart attack occurred as he was cooking for the Catholic High School athletic banquet. He didn't have much money, so he gave of himself.

In the eulogy, Reverend Labit, who had known Daddy when Daddy was a child, said:

"Often the Good Lord takes the best first – children, young mothers, young fathers."

He said this was the case with Sidney Ourso, "one of our best."

At the graveside he put a hand on my shoulder and said, "It's up to you now." By this, I understood him to mean I was to carry on Daddy's business, to take over the management of the funeral home my father had owned.

As Reverend Labit walked away, I felt the sun's warm weight on my shoulder where his hand had been. And I felt the weight of duty to my family. I grieved the loss of my father, but home felt good after the fighting in Europe.

Shortly after the funeral, Daddy's partner decided to go into business for himself. He offered to sell Mother his half.

"I'm sorry, Amy, I've got to strike out on my own," he told her.

Mother understood, but that meant it was up to me alone to provide for my mother and to care for my younger brother, Falcon, and sister, Elsie, who would have to complete their educations. Mother set about opening a flower shop one block from the funeral home.

At LSU, before the war interrupted my studies, I was training to be a sports journalist. I was much encouraged in this direction when I was named a Collegiate All American Sports Editor. Funeral home director was not on my list of preferred careers, though for a while I'd worked for the Biology Department as keeper of the cadaver, which entailed cleaning up after the dissection efforts of human anatomy classes. No other student wanted the job. But, given Daddy's occupation, they figured I'd take it. They offered me $50 a month. I told them I couldn't do it for that. They said, "$75." I said, "No." We agreed at $100. I didn't foresee that in a few years I'd follow in Daddy's footsteps.

At the age of twenty-four, just out of the Army, career choices considerably narrowed by family circumstances, here I was in the springtime of my life, up against it. Daddy's erstwhile partner took the home's two employees with him. He and my father hadn't even owned the building.

My brother, Falcon, graduated from high school that year and together, as partners, we went into the funeral home business. I put up $5,000, Mother put up $5,000 for Falcon, and we bought the old house at 134 Houmas Avenue and remodeled it: air conditioning; tasteful furniture in the coffee room; new carpets. We had to contract for the embalming and limousine services. Mother supplied flowers. All of this gave our profit margins a close shave.

Nights I read. I read Russell Conwell's *Acres of Diamonds* again and again. In it a man travels the world looking for riches; he comes home to find diamonds on his own farm.

Were my acres of diamonds to be found here in Donaldsonville?

I also read about acquisitions. Falcon and I endured the slow, hot summer. The air conditioning worked overtime, as did Falcon and I. In the fall things got a little better: We hired our first employee.

Margy remained very much on my mind. She had never really been out of mind since T. Royal Casso introduced us five years earlier. All through the march north in Europe with Patton to the Battle of the Bulge and Bastogne, she stayed with me. Through the snow and the mud and the smoke and artillery's boom-boom-boom, she was on my mind.

After Daddy's funeral, I looked her up to renew our acquaintance. Of course, the Margy I first saw standing beside T. Royal in the theater had grown up a lot by the time I went into the service. And when I got back, I hadn't seen Margy for three and a half years. By then she was quite a young lady - engaged, as I've said, to marry Dr. Frank Heard.

In Germany with Floyd Roberts, I'd inquire about Margy.

"How's your little cousin doing? Hear anything from home about her?"

By then Margy had graduated from high school and was helping her parents with their business in White Castle. And she was, as Floyd informed me more than once, engaged.

"Oh, Ous, forget Margy. She's engaged," Floyd would say.

"Engaged?" I'd say. "Come on. Who's she engaged to?"

"Ous, forget that girl. She's engaged to a dentist from New Orleans. You haven't got a prayer," Floyd would say.

Floyd's mother - who was Margy's Aunt Bod - had already embroidered the towels, sheets and pillowcases. My heart sank down to the floor at the thought of those embroidered items with another man's initials on them. But I thought, *Well, maybe she'll change her mind. There's still time. Still hope. You never know what can happen.* Still, I was discouraged.

"What's his name?" I'd ask.

Floyd would grin.

"Dr. Heard, Dr. Frank Heard from New Orleans, a big city boy. He's opening a practice in Lake Charles. Ous, forget her. Those pillowcases have a 'F.H.' not an 'E.O.'"

But I wouldn't forget her. I couldn't forget her.

My first summer home from the war, Floyd's brother, Gerald, got married at the Catholic Church in White Castle. Floyd, who had flown back for the wedding, got me an invitation. For the occasion

I bought my first civilian suit, all-season, navy blue.

Margy was to be a bridesmaid. Fortunately for me, her fiancee – who had set up his dentistry practice in Lake Charles – couldn't make it. He should have put forth more effort. But Frank was laid back. Charm wasn't his long suit. Also, he wasn't Catholic, and this was to be a big Catholic wedding. All of these circumstances favored my cause.

Margy was beautiful in her bridesmaid's blue velvet gown. Sweat trickled down my back under my starched white shirt. The Mass and the wedding itself occurred somewhere in my peripheral vision. I was focused on Margy, totally. Margy was escorted down the aisle by a groomsman, passing by like a cool, blue, velvet breeze. Whew! Did she glance green-eyed in my direction? Lord help me. She was so beautiful. Her brown hair, streaked with premature silver, only made her stand out more. Maybe the word is "striking." I was struck. A powerful certainty seized me: *Today is my chance.*

I watched Margy, now standing up with the other bridesmaids, now escorted back up the aisle, now getting her picture taken with the wedding party outside the church. What a picture! They stood on the steps of White Castle's old wooden Catholic Church, smiling, squinting as they faced the glare of the sun. In that picture Margy smiles for me. The picture is still framed in my heart.

The wedding reception was at Italian Hall, a ramshackle wood-frame, one-story building, where the St. Joseph Society frequently held fund-raiser dances on Catholic holidays. Margy's whole family was there, including her many aunts. The aunts stood out in full force on the worn hardwood dance floor, holding sway amidst the rainbow of crepe paper and balloons and food- and drink-laden tables.

Margy's Aunt Bod (everyone referred to her as *Taunte* Bod) stood stoutly by the punch bowl, dipper at the ready. In addition, there were *Tauntes* Olamphe and Cecile (who was called "Sis"); Doris, the youngest of the aunts; Lucille, Bessie and Alice; and others whose names I forget. I decided I would dance with several of the aunts, to see if I could acquire some inside information concerning my prospects with Margy.

I began with the preeminent and very formidable *Taunte* Bod. You could tell by her manner that she carried the most weight, figuratively and literally. Let me tell you, she was rotund, refrigerator size. I said a quick prayer and stood before her. With a flourish of the dipper, she spoke to me.

"Would you like some punch?"

"No ma'am. I'd much rather have the pleasure of this dance with you," I said, putting on my best Cajun charm.

Taunte Bod cast a skeptical eye upon me. Oh, she knew I was up to something. Was she calculating my motives? After due deliberation, she agreed to dance.

"Well, why not? I'd be pleased."

She set the dipper on the table and took the arm I offered, and we walked to the center of the dance floor. The corner of my eye caught Margy, off to one side of the bandstand, watching, wondering. *Taunte* Bod and I assumed the dance position and shuffled off to strains of Glenn Miller in what I hoped passed for a two-step.

"So, young man," *Taunte* Bod began. "You're a friend of Floyd's?"

"Yes, ma'am," I said. "In Germany, we were with General Patton at the siege of Bastogne."

She nodded.

"Ma'am, I want to ask you a direct question."

Here, her eyebrows went up a bit, as if to say direct questions were just her cup of tea.

"Ma'am," I began again, looking her straight in her green eyes, "I want to know what you'd think if your niece, Margy, for whom I have developed an affection, were to change her mind and break her engagement? Would I be an acceptable candidate?"

Taunte Bod was silent for a few moments, deliberating. By now our two-step had become a sort of stationary shuffle. At last she spoke up, with a bit of a smirk.

"Candidate?"

"For Margy's affection."

"Well, E.J.," she said, "now *if* Margy were to change her mind – *if*, mind you – I expect that would be up to Margy herself. But I must emphasize that Margy's engaged to marry Frank Heard, the dentist. I've embroidered the sheets myself. 'F. H.' in big letters."

"Yes, I know that," I said.

That was enough for me. Her reply encouraged me a great deal. If Margy changed her mind, *Taunte* Bod would not stand in my way.

"Thank you," I said.

By then Glenn Miller had come to an end. I escorted *Taunte* Bod back to her spot by the punch bowl.

"Thank you," I said again.

She smiled. Did she wink? With Frank Heard in Lake Charles, I had a chance. I walked toward *Taunte* Cecile.

And so I danced with each of Margy's aunts. With *Taunte* Cecile it was another two-step to the music of Stan Kenton. With *Taunte* Doris it was the jitterbug. And with each of the aunts I received the same reply. *If* Margy were to change her mind, well that would be up to Margy herself. They boosted my spirits considerably. I thought I had charmed the aunts. My heart did a little jitterbug of its own.

By now, I believed Margy could change her mind, and that belief got transformed in my head into the firm conviction that she would. Margy, smiling, still stood off to the side of the band. Did she know what I was about, and did she approve? I hoped so.

After I had danced with the last of the aunts, *Taunte* Alice, I went over and asked Margy for the next dance. This she granted. Her sly smile said, "Yes, and I know you've been up to something." She blushed a little but offered no comment, which I took as a good sign. We had become good friends, and maybe something more, while I was at LSU, so all in all I thought I had reason to hope that she might indeed change her mind. Her silence on the subject of Dr. Heard suggested he was in White Castle much less than he ought to have been – in her eyes, as well as in those of her aunts. Of course, I was jumping the gun. I hadn't, after all, proposed to her. But she could see where I was headed, and she did not discourage my attentions, which surely she would have done if she had no doubts about Frank Heard.

It turned out that the day of Margy's cousin's wedding was truly my day of opportunity. As the reception was winding down, Margy, with whom I danced all of the remaining dances, invited me to the family gathering at her parents' house, for sandwiches and other snacks.

"I'm not a family member," I said, hoping she'd open a window on that prospect.

She ran off to ask her mother's permission that I join them and returned immediately with an affirmative answer. My heart leapt with joy.

Margy's parents' home on Main Street in White Castle, which I now entered for the first time, blew me away. So large and elegant. There were rooms and rooms and rooms, all lavishly furnished, a dining room set, a living room set, bedroom sets. A Steinway baby grand piano with real ivory keys sat right in the living room. Margy, who had taken lessons for years, loved music. I envisioned a beautiful child at the piano in the lavish living room, playing, playing, playing.

Indeed Margy's parents, Philip and Cecile Barbier, owned a home that spoke volumes about what is possible through persistent, hard work, even for people like me, who started from scratch. It stood as an emblem of astonishing success. Only in America!

Margy's family were nice people, considerate people, who made me feel welcome.

"Have another sandwich, E.J.," *Taunte* Bod said. "You must be hungry."

I took a chicken salad sandwich, one of those nice little quarter sandwiches professional caterers prepare. This seemed to please her. *Taunte* Olamphe talked to me about her children. *Taunte* Bessie wanted to know all about the war in Europe.

Margy's father quizzed me about the funeral home business. Did I have plans for expansion? Had I considered getting my own limousine service? Here was a man from whom I could learn. I listened to what he said, and to what he didn't say.

Then after a while, when all the younger generation set out for a club in nearby Napoleonville, Margy insisted I go, too. What a perfect day! Frank Heard's doomsday, but a great day for Eucharist Joseph Ourso. A whole day with Margy. I was totally swept away, way out, no land in sight, in an ocean of love.

I visited with Margy quite a bit during the ensuing weeks. Of course, Falcon and I had the funeral home business to run. Margy's dad had given me much to think about. Listening to him had convinced me that Russell Conwell, author of *Acres of Diamonds*, was absolutely right about what's to be found in your own backyard.

"Falcon," I said, "It's right here, waiting for us."

Falcon looked puzzled.

"Opportunity," I said.

Margy raised my spirits so that everything I saw spoke to me of opportunity. The good life was right here. I devoted every spare moment to Margy. Frank Heard didn't have a chance. Fortunately, his practice kept him in Lake Charles. Clearly Margy's mind was inclining in my direction. I saw it in her green eyes.

Still, she hesitated to break the engagement outright. What was she waiting for? She spoke of her intention to her mother, who passed it along to the council of aunts.

Deliberation was in order. The breaking of an engagement was not to be taken lightly. Here Divine Providence came into play. It came in with those towels, sheets and pillowcases embroidered "F.H." by Margy's *Taunte* Bod. It assumed the form of *Taunte* Bod's deliberative and imaginative powers. Thank the Lord for *Taunte* Bod.

The aunts held a meeting to discuss Margy's engagement to Frank Heard. I received this account from Margy, who got it straight from *Taunte* Bod. First, after all my attentions, all of the aunts but *Taunte* Bod voted against Margy's breaking the engagement.

"She can't change her mind now," they said. "All of her trousseau – the sheets and the pillowcases and the towels – is already embroidered in twelve-inch letters with 'F.H.' How can she break off the engagement now? What will we do with all those linens and towels?"

But then *Taunte* Bod stood up.

"Let's don't be hasty," she said. "Why should Margy ruin her life by marrying someone she does not love? Someone who does not appear to be strongly attached to her? If she does that, she'll end up divorced. Why should we force her to do that?"

As for the sheets and pillowcases and towels, she could fix that.

"All it takes is a little imagination," she said. "Just add a bar at the bottom of the "F" making it an "E" and take the middle bar out of the "H" and replace it with one at the top and one at the bottom, making it an "O".

Divine Providence. If my name had been Winston Churchill, or Jack Kennedy, or Tyrone Power, I wouldn't have won.

On October 9, 1947, Margy and I were married in the old wooden church in White Castle, which we thought fitting since it was there that we had really begun our courtship. Margy's parents held the reception at their elegant home. There must have been three hundred people at our wedding. Margy in her wedding gown was beautiful beyond description. We drove to New Orleans for our honeymoon. Dinner at Antoine's, then dancing. We had the time of our young lives.

Motivation to succeed:
Five little mouths to feed

You want to know *why* marrying Margy was the best business decision – the best decision, period – I ever made?

Because Margy proved to be a super motivator – in more ways than one.

Fertility ran in Margy's family, on both sides, like the Mississippi River in flood season. In less than five years, we had five children. First, ten months after we married, there was Cecile, named for Margy's mother. Eleven months after that Margy had twins: a black-haired boy we named Sidney and a red-haired girl we named Cindy. Twenty-seven months later came Philip, named for Margy's father. And a year after that, Nancy. Good Lord! Five babies in less than five years. And it was my job to bring home enough of a paycheck to feed all these hungry little mouths. To say only that I was deeply motivated would be an understatement.

The apartment we rented in Donaldsonville when we were married proved to be just big enough to hold us and one baby. When the twins were born, we had to pack up and move to a larger apartment. But with two more babies that apartment, too, filled to bursting. I was up to my ears in bottles and diapers, boiling and washing. Margy's department was feeding, except at night when I'd get up to give a bottle, or change a diaper.

We cooked carrots or beets or potatoes and then mashed and strained them. We boiled and cooked and mashed and strained and fed and then started boiling and cooking and mashing and straining all over. Margy was a full-time mother, full-time-and-a-half.

By day I was the young president of the funeral home business, by night the chief cook and bottle washer. In addition to that, we'd added ambulance service. Guess who the backup ambulance driver was.

In the midst of all this, we launched the burial insurance business, starting out with about $8,500 I'd saved from Army pay and what we got from the sale of Margy's one hundred shares of Sears stock. With $10,000 capital, we fancied we were ready to go up against the big boys, Metropolitan and Prudential.

We sold insurance for the services we provided. We made those services affordable to people who otherwise might not be able to afford them, by selling the insurance on an installment plan of a nickel a week. Of course, collecting meant twenty stops to the dollar. I wore holes in the soles of my shoes, which filled up with dirt from the dirt roads and backyards of Donaldsonville. You'd have thought I spent my days digging for diamonds. In a way, I did.

I had discovered a niche. Metropolitan and Prudential had stopped selling insurance on the weekly installment plan. But there were people out there who didn't think they could afford insurance if they had to make a big payment. Right after the war, people who weren't wealthy didn't have $25 all at once. But they did have a nickel a week. A nickel a week didn't seem like a huge amount of money. They couldn't imagine themselves making a big payment every three or six months, but they could imagine themselves paying a nickel a week. Unless someone offered it, they would end up without the services provided by a nice funeral home. Sooner or later these services are needed by everyone. For someone willing to walk, here was opportunity. With five hungry babies, I was willing.

We thought we were in good shape, until the Commissioner of Insurance called me in and told me we would have to close down. I didn't understand.

"Your cash reserve is $1.25, Mr. Ourso," he said, putting out his cigar.

But we had a $10,000 reserve. That was going to cover my salary, and so on.

No, he said, if I dipped into that, my business would be "impaired." He was going to have to close me down. The reserve couldn't be used for operations.

Tears pushed into my eyes.

"No, sir, you can't close me down. I've got a wife and three babies and another one on the way. Do what you want to me. But don't close me down. I don't want my children to grow up hearing that their daddy was a quitter."

I told him I'd give up my $250 a month salary.

"We'll eat potatoes," I told him.

"Okay," he said, "We'll see."

We ate potatoes, which we bought in hundred-pound sacks for a dollar a sack. We ate potatoes mashed, French fried, baked, scalloped, and hashed. Potatoes for breakfast, lunch, and dinner, for what seemed like forever, but was actually three months. Margy never complained.

Meanwhile, the necessity of success weighed heavily upon me. All the infant formula, and diapers, and little shoes, and doctor's bills. I *had* to succeed.

Many a night I woke with the weight of the world on my chest, squeezing the breath out of me. *Where would I get the money for the week's payroll?* My beautiful green-eyed bride would reach through the heavy darkness and touch my shoulder, my chest.

"We'll make it. Don't worry, Ous, we're going to make it."

Her touch gave me back my breath. Every time she got me through. She wouldn't let me quit.

Mornings I rose from bed with one thought: *Ous, get out there and sell policies.* I looked at myself shaving in the mirror. *Ous, it's up to you.* Diamonds in Donaldsonville? It takes a lot of stops at a nickel a stop. There were setbacks, discouragements, defeats. My competitors got to my customers. On my rounds, I sometimes saw my policies impaled on picket fences. My heart would sink, and tears would push into my eyes. My face was back on the canvas. *Hamburger Ourso, get up, get up.* Five hungry babies kept my focus on selling. *Ous, get up and knock the sonofabitch out.* The holes in my shoes grew huge.

When Philip was born we moved into a bungalow. It gave us a bit more room, and, with business picking up, we hired a nanny to help Margy with the twins. A middle-aged woman who spoke only French, she was a blessing. She stayed with us four years. The post-World War II boom was booming by then. Margy and I were into the baby boom. The Great Depression was over. The war was over. No more rationing gasoline and sugar. Margy and I had a car, though I still walked when I did my debit routes, i.e., when I went around to my customers' houses to collect premiums. I had a new pair of shoes.

Sundays we drove. Margy and I and the children piled into the Chevy and drove to see the countryside. Like other young couples with growing families, we looked at houses and dreamed. The finest house in town, to our eyes, was owned by a prominent lawyer, Walter Lemann. It was a big four-story house set on a lot a block long and half a block wide, on the corner of Iberville Street and Lee Avenue. We dreamed about renovating it. It had beautiful French doors and windows along the Lee side. All that light and space.

The big yard had great appeal. The children could run without running out of sight. Sidney, a climber, liked the trees. The perfect house for us.

"Margy, one day I'm going to buy you that house," I'd say as we coasted by.

If I had said to anyone else in town that I intended one day to live in the Lemann's grand house, they'd have locked me up. That was before it was even for sale.

Walter Lemann died in 1952. By then their children were grown and rearing families of their own. Like so many, they had probably moved away to seek employment. So Mrs. Lemann lived alone, with little to occupy her time except her weekly game of *bourrée* with ladies at her club. She must have rambled about in that huge house, meeting only ghosts. She wanted to get out. Our dream house went up for sale: $50,000.

In 1952 not many people in Donaldsonville had that much money. The house was worth it, but it was more than we could afford. For whatever reason, there were no takers. The "For Sale" sign stayed in the front yard for months. Sundays Margy and I and the children coasted by, holding our breath, hearts jumping for fear we'd see a "Sold" sign.

"Still there," we'd whisper. "Still there."

I heard about Mrs. Lemann's situation from two of her card-playing friends.

"She's anxious to sell. Make her an offer," one of them said.

With an FHA loan we could offer $20,000, so we did. And she accepted. Margy was ecstatic, as was I. A house of our own, spare rooms. But our family expanded to fill the space. Nine months after we moved in, Nancy was born. And after a while, Lori.

We did not seek our diamonds elsewhere. We stayed home in Donaldsonville.

Margy liked the children within sight, or at least within hearing, so she invited the neighborhood kids to our yard. The constant pounding of little feet beat that yard down till it looked like a school yard. The boys, Sidney and Philip, were especially hard on it, but the girls weren't easy on it either.

The next door neighbor thought we'd started a kindergarten. He wasn't happy. Nor did the boys lighten his mood when they built a tree house over by his yard and, in hooking up lights, tapped into his electricity. Lord, how they didn't get electrocuted, I don't know. What would they do next?

Well, we figured, if that's the worst, we're doing okay. And by then, all things considered, we really were.

I straightened out the electric bill with our neighbor.

CHAPTER 2

Never Forget Where You Came From

T HE OFFICE I WORK IN NOW, ON THE SECOND
floor of the house on St. Charles Avenue, is four times the size
of my first office on the west end of Iberville Street in
Donaldsonville.

Here twice a week I meet with Jesse Arboneaux and Cathy LeBlanc,
who come down from Donaldsonville on Tuesdays and Thursdays to
bring me the weekly business – checks to be signed, decisions to be
made, a detailed report on how things are going. Jesse and Cathy have
been with me for more than a quarter of a century. My Donaldsonville
connection.

Hardworking country people. Cathy was born in Donaldsonville and
reared in the nearby community of Brusly McCall; she started with me
at age eighteen. Jesse, from Napoleonville, has lived in Donaldsonville
since the early 1970s. Give me country people, who have grown up
with hard work, who were taught to value accomplishment from when
they were little. They're family.

My office is in the house's north corner; its windows provide a view
of the green leaves of the venerable Louisiana live oaks that grow in the
yard. Squirrels and crows have colonized this urban territory. Their
presence reminds me that once all this was theirs, and we, in their eyes,
are the interlopers. They go about their business, paying me no mind.

From this vantage point New Orleans is a glimpse of neighboring
rooftops and the grind of the streetcars on St. Charles Avenue. The bell

of the Episcopalian Church across the street tolls at noon. But in here, amid the heavy furniture and solid African mahogany woodwork, sitting at my table or standing at the window looking down at the squirrels darting about in the yard, at age seventy-eight, I am still a Donaldsonville boy.

I was born on June 16, 1923 in my parents' house on the banks of Bayou Lafourche, two miles out of Donaldsonville. I was the first of three children. Mother told the story over and over of how Minnie, the elderly black midwife who lived nearby, delivered me from the womb.

"When you were born, you were blue, blue from head to toe. 'Lord help me,' I said when I saw you. I wasn't but twenty, and with a blue baby. Minnie knew exactly what to do. She pinched your cheeks and she spit in your mouth, and the natural healthy color came into your face and limbs, and you howled."

For Minnie it was all in a day's work. Mother said a prayer of thanksgiving.

"Minnie was, as sure as I'm standing here, a worker in the employ of Divine Providence," Mother would say.

With that kind of jump start, could I ever forget where I came from? It all comes with me, follows me about, hangs on with me here on St. Charles Avenue. It's in my sweat and blood, in my flesh and bones.

Donaldsonville. To go there, get off I-10 on your way from Baton Rouge to New Orleans at the Sorrento/Donaldsonville exit, turn left on La. Hwy. 70 and go on over the Sunshine Bridge, which crosses the Mississippi River. Drive about six miles on Hwy. 70 through the flood plain planted with sugarcane, and, as you enter town, bear right onto what becomes Marchand Street. When you come to Railroad Avenue you're in the heart of the heart of Donaldsonville. The First and Last Chance Café will be off to your left.

In Donaldsonville's heyday, around the turn of the century, the First and Last Chance was your last chance to get a drink before the train headed north to Alexandria and your first chance to get one when it returned to south Louisiana.

But don't stop there now. Go right on Railroad Avenue, past the Chamber of Commerce and the Tourist Office, past the little green town park on your left. The Ourso Management Company occupies the second floor of the old *Donaldsonville Chief* building at 118 Railroad Avenue. It's the two-story brick building across the street from the Elks Club and next door to the old Security Building, my office for years and years, until we sold the company.

Though we sold Security Industrial Insurance, I didn't retire. No, I'm cooking up some ideas, got a thing or two in the pot.

John Folse, Donaldsonville's world famous restaurateur, says that in our town we lived in a food culture. Saturday nights, what was there to do except cook, eat, drink, and dance? Food surrounded us.

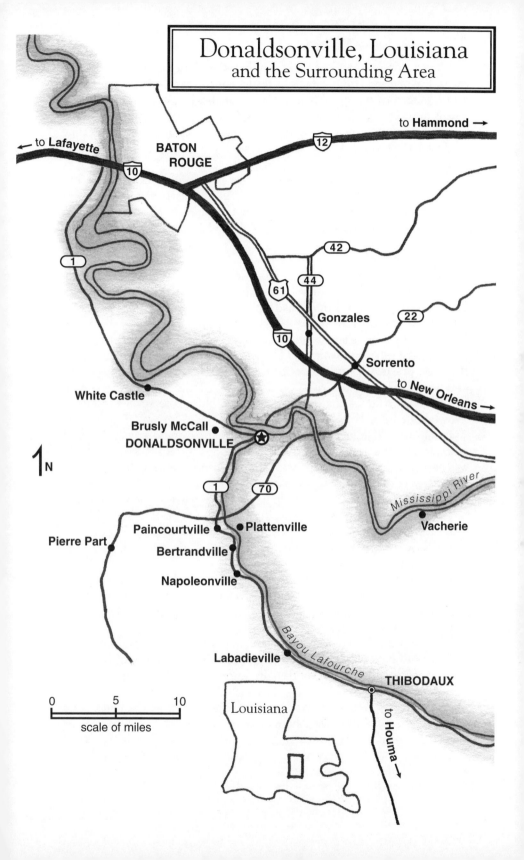

I love to cook – food or ideas. My library's full of cookbooks. As for ideas, I've always been a voracious reader. In the early days, when Margy and I were starting out, I read a book a night. Books like *Acres of Diamonds* and *Think and Grow Rich*. I read how A.P. Giannini built the Bank of America. I read those books over and over and over. Each time I learned something. That's how I cooked up ideas about the insurance business.

Every book had at least a good idea or two. I gobbled them up. I'm a hungry reader still. The world's full of good ideas, every one an opportunity, waiting for someone with the imagination to seize it and the perseverance to make it work.

Talk about cooking, talk about imagination and perseverance, let me tell you about John Folse, one of the world's best chefs. His restaurant, Lafitte's Landing, burned down in 1998. Did that stop him? No. He renovated his own home, made it into a restaurant. Less than a year after the fire, John reopened.

He wasn't a big success when he first got started. But I knew from talking to him he was a winner. The first Lafitte's Landing was down by the river, practically under the Sunshine Bridge. John opened his doors and waited. The town's expert on fine dining. Trouble was, most people in Donaldsonville at that time wanted the blue plate special. Nobody knew about John Folse and fine dining.

Finally, one day he called me and asked if he could come over and talk. He'd always appreciated our conversations. I said, "Come on." He was at my office door in minutes. He described his empty dining room, his empty parking lot, his low cash flow.

"I want to innovate, educate Donaldsonville palates," he proclaimed.

But before he could innovate, he had to survive. He served good food. He greeted customers at the door. If he was nice to them they'd come back. But as things stood, he concluded, he could die cooking good food and being nice.

I didn't say a word, just kicked back from my desk and pointed to the framed cartoon of two buzzards I had hanging on the wall behind me. John read the caption. The one buzzard was saying to the other, "Patience, my ass. I'm going to go out and kill something."

That was all the advice John needed. John got out and started to make things happen, as the buzzard advised. Imagination and perseverance. Now John's an internationally known chef. He's spread south Louisiana cuisine all over the world, including Moscow.

Another Donaldsonville boy who made good is Billy Guillot, young owner of the First and Last Chance Café. The boy who used to cut our lawn now ships about a thousand cases of his famous garlic sauce all over the world nearly every week. Best garlic sauce under the sun. A two and a half million dollar business.

Donaldsonville's had more than its share of entrepreneurs. Success meant you had really done something, because you sure hadn't had much when you started. Maybe growing up poor engenders great desire for success.

Our beginnings occupy us, live with us till those six carry us out. In my case, I remember life as a young boy pulling my wagon loaded with scrap paper or iron through the streets of Donaldsonville. I carry with me that same boy, who went door to door to door to door with twelve live chickens hanging heavy and odorous on a cotton cord around his neck. I can reach back and put my finger on the cord's old crease. I feel, as a high school boy, the light touch of fingers as I take the ticket of my bride-to-be, though I didn't know it then, at the Grand Theatre. Through young eyes, I watch her descend into the darkened, popcorn-flavored theater. All the taste and smell and heat of Donaldsonville is soaked into my pores. I can't sweat it out, can't spit the grit of Donaldsonville summer road dust out of my mouth. I just swallow it and keep going. It's me.

How can I tell this to the MBA students from LSU who come down from Baton Rouge with Professor Bob Justis? They come to talk to me about business. What is my advice on this subject?

"Never forget where you come from."

This is a much neglected principle of business, so I explain it.

"Where you come from is who you are and how you think about yourself. Forget where you come from and you forget who you are, the grit you are made of. Sure, many people forget, or do everything they can to forget. But don't you do it. Don't you deny it. Carry it with you. Make something good of it. It's your opportunity. Success in business, or any other line of endeavor, is tied up with who you are. Know who you are."

The Ourso Family's roots

Ourso roots reach deep in Donaldsonville soil, deep down into Donaldsonville's history, to the Spanish who preceded the French. On August 15, 1772, a Spanish priest founded the Ascension Catholic Church at a bend in the Mississippi River in the little settlement that became Donaldsonville. Also in 1772, King Charles III granted to a man named Del Ourse a large tract of land, with riparian rights, stretching from the river to where the community of Brusly McCall is now.

Shortly thereafter, when the French took over the government of the territory that included the present state of Louisiana, they "Frenchified" the old Spanish "Del Ourse" to "Ourso." That distant Spanish progenitor cleared the land and planted corn and vegetables. Later Oursos, under French rule, planted sugarcane.

So, Oursos literally put their roots down all around here before the country's beginning, long, long before the coming of the oil drillers and the manufacturers of fertilizer and chemicals, who now dominate the local economy.

Del Ourse's descendants gave up more than their name to the French. Not understanding the language of the governors, they were forced by the French to give up bit by bit the land Del Ourse had been granted. Under French tax laws, they were easy prey for well-versed French lawyers. Eventually the French weaseled Oursos out of all but scraps of the land grant. By the time my father was born, the Ourso occupation had been reduced to a cottage back in Brusly McCall. It was here that my father, Sidney Ourso, and his brothers and sisters grew up.

Both he and Mother, a Falcon, were plain country people. Mother's people were good, hardworking, country folk from down along Bayou Lafourche. As for the Falcons, you still find Falcons all over Donaldsonville. Mr. and Mrs. Simon Falcon, my maternal grandparents, had eight sons, seven of whom served their country in World War II at the same time.

I mention all this to tell you about these people – the Oursos and the Falcons. Large families, some with twelve children, hardworking, durable, patriotic, Catholic, family people. They put the old French injustice behind them. They looked life straight in the eye and tried to do what had to be done for their God, for their family, for their country. They shared what little they had among themselves and with their neighbors.

The faces that look out at you from old photographs of the Oursos and Falcons bespeak arduous lives. You can also see their determination to make the best of things, to make something good come of their lives, to live them as well as they could, which meant making do for themselves and doing for others as well.

Growing up in the Depression

Mother and Daddy met at a country dance, courted, and married at an early age. Daddy went to work for Standard Oil in Baton Rouge until, when the Depression hit, they wanted to transfer him to Guatemala.

"Guatemala? Lord help us," Mother said. She set her fork by her plate and bowed her head.

"Guatemala or termination," Daddy said.

"What's 'termination,'" I asked.

"It's not good," Daddy said. "It's a kind of end."

"Where's Guatemala?"

"Central America. South of Mexico."

Mother shook her head. Guatemala sounded worse than a kind of end to her. She picked up her fork and began to eat, not inclined to interrupt dinner to go to Guatemala.

"Isn't this our home?" I asked.

"South Louisiana's where we're from," Daddy said. "We'll make do. I'll see what I can do around here. Maybe it's a blessing in disguise."

The work at Standard Oil had worn him down. His real bent was talking with people, helping them, explaining things to them. If you were down, spend a little while with Daddy and you'd feel better.

I for one felt good we weren't going to Guatemala, wherever it was. Mother did, too. Making do sounded better than Guatemala or termination.

For a while Daddy managed Woodruff's Funeral Home in Donaldsonville and sold burial insurance. He would commute from Baton Rouge, where we were living at the time. This suited him better than the hard labor at Standard Oil. But when Woodruff's succumbed to the Depression, Daddy and Mother decided to move back to Donaldsonville. This was in 1933.

For a while we lived in a ramshackle shotgun house about two miles out of Donaldsonville on Bayou Lafourche, but then we moved to Railroad Avenue. The house was bigger and nicer, and you could walk right down its front steps directly to the street.

After about a year, we moved to a big old house on the corner of Houmas Avenue and Iberville Street, scarcely more than three blocks from the Ascension Catholic Church, which we attended every Sunday. Daddy and a partner joined up in the funeral home business. For this purpose, they leased the house we lived in.

We made do.

Despite the Depression we persisted; we persevered. We made do from one day to the next to the next one after that and on and on, each day indistinguishable from the one before it, stretching back in memory so that nothing was ever any different. Time had slowed down, run down like an old car out of gas, coasting to a stop on a hot, dusty road. And now the people were out of the car and standing around talking about what to do.

Everybody we knew was stuck in the Depression together. FDR – President Franklin D. Roosevelt – was our hope for a new life. Always there were people outdoors in the yards, in the streets, talking about what to do, telling stories, butting into each other's business. Neighbors stopped one another in the street.

"Where are you headed?" they asked one another, as easily as they might say "Good morning."

Depression Donaldsonville was not like the neighborhoods of today's suburbia, where people pretty much keep to themselves and mind their own business. No, in Donaldsonville, as well as in Napoleonville, Pierre Part, Paincourtville, White Castle, Plattenville, Brusly McCall and Vacherie, everybody became fully informed about everybody. And just in case you might miss something, you could go and sit in the beauty parlor owned by Marie Cecile Landry, also known as "The Source" (pronounced "Sosse"), and catch up on the very latest news and gossip.

The *Donaldsonville Chief* was no match for the "Sosse" when it came to local coverage. Why, if you had been a fly on the wall at this beauty parlor, you'd have found out things you didn't know about yourself.

Mother, for one, loved to tell stories, especially about her children. She told over and over the story about how I helped to make do. In her story we were still on Railroad Avenue in the house with the porch steps that went right down to the street, where people passed by all day long. Mother said:

"The closeness of the street must have given him an idea. He took all the broken toys he could find, his, or Falcon's, or Elsie's, whatever none of them wanted – a torn doll, a baby's rattle that didn't rattle, a ball with a hole in it, a scooter with one wheel. He arranged them on the steps, as though they were toys on shelves in a store. He intended to sell them.

"He worked at it for days out there, hot sun beating down on his head. He wouldn't get discouraged. We couldn't get him to quit.

"I carried him a pitcher of lemonade, which he took to offering in little paper cups to the people passing by. He figured if he could get people to pause for a cool drink, while they were paused maybe they'd see something they wanted. The lemonade was free.

"Let me tell you. A Negro lady with a small boy came by and looked at the ball that had a hole in it. She said, 'Why, that ball's got a hole in it. What good is a ball with a hole in it?'"

Mother would tell how I held the ball out to the small boy, so he could hold it in his own hand, as if it were his. If he liked it, his mother would buy it. Mother would continue:

"E.J. said, straight out, not batting an eye, 'Ma'am, get that ball for your boy, and you won't have to worry about him breaking it. He can't break it.' And then he asked the boy, 'You like it?' You know, she bought that ball. The little boy didn't care about the hole. This was his first ball. It didn't bounce, but it rolled. E.J. looks at people and knows what they'll want. Lord knows where he gets it. It's a gift."

What pleasure Mother took in that story!

At the "Sosse," my reputation as a businessman was assured at the tender age of eight or so. Never mind that I had long, hard miles to go. She told that story long after I had grown. It became a defining event of my youth, foreshadowing the entrepreneurial direction my life was to take. I came to believe I was an entrepreneur, the way you come to believe something if you hear it enough.

Mother told that story to Father Labit at Daddy's funeral. Father Labit's predecessor, Father Chambon, heard it when he came to dinner, as he often did at Daddy's invitation. Mother would tell it to customers who came to her flower shop.

In Donaldsonville the Depression was a time of intense closeness, a time when no one had much except each other. So there were Sundays, after church, when just about everybody we knew, which took in pretty much everyone in town, was out on the banks of Bayou Lafourche, catching crawfish and boiling them with potatoes and corn.

You didn't wait to be invited to these spontaneous town picnics. In fact, nobody was invited. Everyone just expected you to be there. If you weren't, people thought you were sick and inquired about your health.

What a crowd. Everywhere there were children yelling, dogs barking, mothers with baby carriages, fathers throwing balls with their sons. All around, green shimmered in bright sunlight. No rain in sight. We couldn't hear the far off rumbling thunder of my generation's great war.

Acres of Diamonds
in my own backyard

M aking do.
In 1933 I was ten years old, a collector of scrap paper, scrap iron, and bone for buttons, long before the *Chief*'s headline - "Lack of scrap could lose this War" - rendered such pursuits patriotic.

Mainly I collected old newspapers. Everyone had old newspapers. Iron was better but harder to come by. Somebody might want to throw away an old stove or an icebox battered beyond use - but rarely.

Bones were like buried treasure. For them I had to tramp up and down in Granddaddy Falcon's pasture in the hopes of coming across the ant- and beetle-cleaned carcass of a long-dead cow or pig.

Elray Kocke Service, Inc. paid two cents a hundred pounds for the paper, twice that for the iron, and eight cents a hundred pounds for bones. Elray Kocke's main business was providing and hauling oil mud and equipment, so they had trucks that they also used to haul scrap or, for that matter, to move a household. In the Depression they weren't particular about what it was as long as it needed moving, just as I wasn't particular about what I collected just as long as I could turn around and sell it.

The Depression days taught you to do what you could; not to be choosy. Hustling newspaper, iron and bone was harder work by far than peddling broken toys from your doorstep. But the cash flow was better. You had to get out and "look around the corner" a bit, instead of waiting for the world to walk by. Those comic buzzards in the cartoon that came to hang on my office wall reiterated this lesson.

I collected the newspapers, iron and bones and stacked them in an old four-wheel wagon made of wood, the kind children are given to pull about. Even its wheels were wooden. It was hard to pull, especially when loaded with a stack of newspapers up to my chest, which was about its limit.

Pulling that weight, on the wooden wheels, was slow, hard, creaking labor for a skinny boy of ten, but I persisted. Every hot summer day, the heavy air pressing down off the Mississippi, lifting the dust up off the dirt and gravel roads, I trudged up and down Donaldsonville's sad

Depression era streets. Most of the streets were unpaved, and if it had rained they were covered with mud that greatly impeded my efforts.

"Ma'am, do you have any old papers? Anything at all made of iron you don't want? Any old bones?" They gave me what they had, just to have it hauled away. There were never any bones they'd admit to.

For school children, the summer of 1933 was longer than all others because a lack of money compelled the schools to close nearly two months early. When the money ran out, they simply turned us loose.

But in the Depression, summers weren't just for having fun. Summers, even to ten-year-old boys, were opportunities to earn money, opportunities to help make do. As my parents' oldest child, I was expected to do something to earn money.

For me it was a way to earn respect. In the Depression if you could figure out how to earn money, people respected you. I could see respect in my father's eyes when I put my nickels and dimes and quarters on the kitchen table in the evening.

The competition for scrap got fierce. Every enterprising school boy released from the tedium of the classroom was out with his wagon making his rounds. Donaldsonville must have had nearly a thousand school children, so it took only a couple of months for what had been a torrent of scrap newspaper to diminish to a thin trickle. The competition for the iron was even fiercer, because it was scarcer. As spring wore into summer, it got harder and harder to bring home the nickels, dimes, and quarters.

In May I had been able to load up my wagon with papers in less than two hours. In a morning I might make three hauls over to Elray's. If I could do the same in the afternoon, I could make as much as fifty cents a day. If I got iron, I might get a whole dollar from the scrap yard man. Bone days were easy money days – maybe a dollar and a half or two dollars, if I got lucky.

But come July I was doing well to get a load of newspapers a day. As for scrap iron, lots of luck. People didn't buy appliances much in the Depression. They kept what they had and tried to fix it. Whatever scrap iron people had had was long since collected.

My need drove me further and further toward the outskirts of town, way down dusty dirt and gravel roads – with little hope of success. The flow of cash – the quarters and dimes and nickels I'd been putting on the kitchen table each evening for my parents and brother and sister to admire – diminished and finally stopped.

Daddy understood how I felt. Evenings when I was at a low point, he'd touch my shoulder and smile. He knew I was out there day in and day out hustling. At church, sometimes, I prayed for help.

Many a night I lay in my bed, in the dark room I shared with Falcon, thinking wishfully. My imagination pictured stacks and stacks of newspapers, stashes containing years of papers, back to Donaldsonville's beginning. They were stacked to the rafters – papers not only from

Donaldsonville, but from all the major cities of Louisiana: Baton Rouge, New Orleans, Lafayette, Lake Charles, Alexandria. I imagined magazines, years and years of *Time* and *National Geographic* and *Saturday Evening Post*.

And at the same time, as though I was watching two movies at the Grand Theatre at once, I saw all sorts of iron objects, objects like old farm implements and pipes and sprocket wheels with cogs from decomposed sugar mills like the works of a giant clock. There was an ancient anvil that must have weighed a ton. There were things I didn't recognize, but I knew they were iron.

It was a dream treasure, the dream of a boy whose every thought for the previous two months had focused on the collection of scrap newspaper and unwanted iron.

Now, in the dream I thought, as if it were a dream about a dream, if I can dream all this, I must have seen it somewhere, because I couldn't dream it all up out of absolutely nothing. It's out there somewhere. I'd turn a corner and see it. But which corner?

Lord help me, I thought. *Where have I seen these treasures?*

Then it came to me!

The newspapers, magazines and old iron, they filled the attics and backyard sheds of Donaldsonville. This stuff was everywhere!

In the predawn dark I sat up awake with a huge vision that took in all the newspaper-stuffed attics and iron-filled sheds in town. A vision real enough to reach out and touch, it smelled of old dust and oil, had the feel of sharp edges and rust.

First hint of light, before my family was stirring, before the first backyard rooster crowed, I had my wagon on the move on Railroad Avenue.

"Ma'am," I said to our sleepy next door neighbor, "do you need your attic cleaned? I'll clean your shed in the back, too."

You can bet people who've lived long in a house have been piling up junk they don't quite know what to do with in their attics and sheds for years and years till it's so bad they can't face it. This was my opportunity.

"I'll clean them out for you. Free. If you'll let me have the newspapers. And any old stuff, heavy old useless iron, in the shed you don't want. I'll haul it away, free."

The neighbor looked at me the way older people look at something they can't quite see without their glasses. Through the door's dusty screen, she made out a skinny boy in short pants with a wagon in tow standing on the back doorstep. She blinked. Was she dreaming? Would this boy from next door really clean out her attic and shed? Just for the papers and scrap iron he could carry away? What a bargain!

Who wants to go up to clean an unbearably hot attic in the middle of a Louisiana summer? Not her. Not her husband she'd been after for years to do something about that shed. Lord, it was about to fall down anyway. An eyesore.

"Me, I'll do it, ma'am, for free, if I can have all the old paper. If I can haul off the old iron. Free."

She nodded a sleepy "yes" and led me through the house, past the bedroom with her sleeping husband tangled in the sheets, to the attic.

From just one attic, I got whole wagonloads of newspapers, some of them forty years old. All the newspapers and magazines of my dreams and more were there. And not only years of *Time* and *National Geographic* but also of *Harper's*, *The Atlantic Monthly*, and *Saturday Evening Post* stacked right up to the rafters. It took more than a dozen wagonloads, back and forth, back and forth, back and forth from Elray's. I feared I would wear out my creaking wagon wheels.

The next day I returned at daybreak to tackle the shed, which had more old useless iron in it than I'd seen in one place except for Elray's junkyard. The shed took two days' solid work. I loved it. And, yes, in it stood the anvil from my dreams. The neighbor got her husband up to help me load it on my wagon, which nearly collapsed under its weight.

Elray Kocke's man couldn't believe it.

"Where you finding all these papers," he demanded. "Hell, kid, you discover an iron mine?"

"I dreamed it," I said with a smirk.

The quarters, dimes and nickels dropped into my cupped hands. At home, the eyes of my mother, father, brother, and sister widened as I poured my treasure onto the kitchen table. Coins rolled everywhere.

"In a depression, our boy is going to be a millionaire," my mother said. She put her arms out across the table to keep the coins from rolling off onto the floor.

Daddy shook his head.

"Well done, son. How did you do it?" he asked.

"Dreams. I dreamed it."

He looked a little hurt, turned the corners of his mouth down and tilted his head back, as if to say, "Well, go on and be like that." But he was proud of me. It gave my self-esteem a boost.

I didn't need to wait for Russell Conwell to tell me about the acres of diamonds in my own backyard.

I was on to something. Strike while the iron is hot, they say. Don't talk to anybody about it, just work. The Depression taught that. Take what work you can get and do it. Pennies, nickels, dimes, quarters add up to dollars. Daddy told me about saving up for a rainy day. This was more cash than we needed right then. He took me to the First National Bank of Donaldsonville, just then getting chartered as a national bank.

"If you put that money in this bank," he explained, "it will grow. That is, the bank will pay you, just to let them keep your money for you. It's called earning interest."

"They'll pay me? How much?"

I began to learn about the power of interest, particularly compound interest. Power, if you've got time. That's what I tell the MBAs: "You're young and have plenty of time."

Just by putting my money in the bank it would grow, not real fast, not at first. I thought of the lifting and hauling I had to do to earn eight cents. Earning interest meant I could earn something without all that. It just happened. Of course, I understood that you had to work to put money in the bank. It wasn't free money, but it was truly like a dream.

"Just because I let you keep it for me?" I asked the teller.

"Yes, that's how it works," he said.

The teller gave me a little green book with numbers in it telling me how much money I had. A scorecard. I looked back at the teller as we went out through the bank's revolving door, even then not fully believing.

"Well," Daddy explained, out on the street, back in the natural daylight, "they're paying you rent for your money, the way you might pay rent for a bicycle one afternoon and then return it. You like that?"

"Yes."

Each week that summer I took some of the money I earned and went to the bank. I watched the little numbers in my green book go up and up. The teller told me that after six months, if I left the money in the account, the numbers would do a little jump up all on their own, like magic.

About half of the money I brought home went for things we needed: food, clothes, shoes for me and my brother and sister. It didn't seem like much, but Daddy said it was a big help. It also occurred to me that if the bank would pay me just because I put my money there, I could afford to put some money in the collection plate they passed at church on Sundays.

Hadn't I prayed? Hadn't I prayed in my dream for the Lord's help? Hadn't it come? These questions had bobbed to the surface of my mind each Sunday thereafter. If I put something in the plate, as Daddy did each Sunday, well, then it was a way of reminding myself that my good fortune was just that – something, an opportunity, granted to me.

From listening to Father Chambon, I knew money wasn't just for hoarding up. In fact, if you hoarded your treasure, you might be guilty of the sin of cupidity or avarice, whereas giving, sharing what we had, was considered virtuous. As Father Chambon explained it, it was plain common sense even a ten-year-old could understand. If you get help, you give help.

Father Chambon became aware of my putting money in the collection plate every Sunday. He told my mother I was a boy of virtuous habits and that he hoped I might consider the priesthood. When she repeated this to Daddy one evening, he only smiled.

"That would be fine, but he's headed in another direction," Daddy said.

And so I was.

The summer of the
seven hundred chickens

My path in life, its general direction anyway, was established the following summer when my father's sister's husband, Uncle John Cavalier, recruited me – "conscripted" is the more accurate word – to sell his seven hundred chickens.

How could I ever forget the summer of the seven hundred chickens? Twelve live Rhode Island Reds hung about me every day, strung six on my right side and six on my left, upside down on a cotton cord that, in the course of the summer, cut a permanent crease into the back of my neck.

My entrepreneurial display the previous summer had not escaped Uncle John's cunning eye. Likely my story-telling mother spread the word to Uncle John and Aunt Clara during one of their visits to town. A hostler on a farm two miles north of Donaldsonville, Uncle John had charge of the farmer's mules and horses.

But Uncle John, an aspiring entrepreneur himself, had invested in seven hundred Rhode Island Red chicks, which he attempted to discretely house and feed on his employer's farm. That spring he had seven hundred plump, market-ready spring chickens, whose racket of clucking and squawking, unfortunately, could be heard from a great distance, so that a body could hardly get away from it. Feeding them was no trivial matter either.

They distracted John from his duties with the mules and horses, which would bring him no profit beyond his regular wages. The farmer did not fail to notice that his mules and horses seemed to get thinner and thinner while Uncle John's chickens got fatter and fatter.

Out of patience, the farmer sent Uncle John and Aunt Clara packing – along with their seven young children and seven hundred fat chickens squeezed into wood crates. They moved to Donaldsonville, where they rented a house on St. Patrick Street, not far from where we lived. Of course, as soon as they stowed the chicken crates in their backyard, Aunt Clara scurried over to talk to Mother.

"We're practically neighbors now," said Aunt Clara.

She came in and sat down in Mother's parlor and commenced to relate how Uncle John's seven hundred chickens had not only gotten him fired and all of them evicted from their quarters but were now about to eat them out of house and home. Something had to be done. The chickens had to be sold before they got to be "tough old hens nobody wanted," she told Mother.

Uncle John knew only mules and horses. He couldn't sell seven hundred chickens if his life depended on it, which literally, Mother observed afterward, it did.

Mother was not about to turn away her husband's sister and her seven children in their hour of need.

"Why, Clara, I bet E.J. could sell them," Mother said. "He can sell anything. Have I told you about the time he sold a woman a ball with a hole in it for her little boy? Yes, well Lord knows we can't let those chickens eat you out of house and home."

The upshot of it all was that Mother agreed with Uncle John and Aunt Clara that I was the person for the job.

When I got home from school that day, Mother called me aside.

"Uncle John would like to speak to you," she informed me.

She explained how Uncle John and Aunt Clara and the seven kids had to leave the farm with the flock of chickens, now all squeezed into crates.

"What are they going to do with them?" I asked, not really wanting to know.

"Well, that's what Uncle John wants to talk to you about."

So I walked over to Uncle John's and Aunt Clara's house. Let me tell you, chickens are filthy, smelly animals. It didn't require much to figure out which house was theirs.

However, these, as Uncle John explained to me, were not your plain, old barnyard chickens. No, they were fancy, up East-style chickens, if you will: Rhode Island Reds. Almost miraculously, these aristocratic creatures had come into Uncle John's possession.

I sat with Uncle John out back on the top doorstep. Chicken crates were everywhere, the unhappy chickens scratching, pecking, squawking to beat the band. Give them a week and these chickens were going to scratch their way out and tear up every blade of grass in the yard till there was nothing but packed dirt, like a school yard.

The seven kids tramped around down in the yard. Aunt Clara had gone in the door as I came out. She didn't look happy.

For a while Uncle John didn't speak; he just stared out at the chickens as if he'd never seen such marvelous creatures.

"You kids," he said at last, "you be careful not to harm any of those chickens. They're valuable property."

He glanced sideways at me.

"Valuable property," he repeated for my benefit.

I held my silence, not wanting to get myself into something I was starting to sense I didn't want to be in. Uncle John had sweated dark stains into his denim shirt where it stretched over his belly. A wisp of damp hair clung to his forehead.

"E.J.," he said. "Look." He reached a practiced hand in the nearest crate and quick as a snake grabbed a Rhode Island Red by its legs and hauled it out. It blinked slowly in the bright afternoon sunlight.

"E.J., you see this here nice, tender, young spring chicken? It's so young and tender it doesn't even yet have spurs on its legs. Feel how smooth this leg is."

I reached out and felt the scaly chicken leg.

"Yes, sir. Not a bump."

"Here," he said, "grab ahold of both legs, like this." He held the Red upside down and hefted her at arm's length. "Feel the weight of her," he said.

I felt her weight. The Red squawked and beat her wings. I handed her back and he stuck her back in the crate. Uncle John put his sweaty arm over my shoulder.

"*Compadre,*" he began in deference to my Spanish origins, "let me put a proposition to you."

Then he explained how I could sell these seven hundred chickens as easy as pie, right here in Donaldsonville.

"Everybody knows you," he pointed out.

The proposition was that for each chicken I sold, at two bits a pound, he'd pay me a commission of a nickel a pound.

"A nickel a stop," he calculated.

I figured one sale in three stops would be more realistic. No matter, Uncle John wasn't considering such subtleties. He took some cotton cord out of his pocket, grabbed the Red back out of the crate, and showed me how to loop it around the legs and hang it upside down.

"See, like this." The chicken's own weight kept the cord tight around its legs. And then he strung up eleven more and hung the string around his neck.

"Nothing to it," he said. His denim shirt quickly became soiled with chicken vomit and the product of instant diarrhea.

"What do you say, kid? Ain't nothing to it. Think about it, a nickel every stop. Twenty stops to the dollar. Most of these chickens are going to weigh in at better than a pound and a half. Can't beat that, can you?"

A nickel a stop, twenty stops to the dollar. I tried to calculate in my head what it might come to. Well, it all hinged on how many stops you had to make for each chicken sold.

How many stops could I make in a morning? Twenty? More, if I was working in town, where the houses were closer together. People out in the country would already have their own flock of chickens. Still, the deciding factor was that I knew Mother wanted me to help Uncle John and Aunt Clara. Those chickens were eating them up.

So, in the end, I agreed to Uncle John's proposition. But I must say the prospect of trudging around shackled like some kind of agricultural convict with twelve Rhode Island Reds dragged my self-esteem down into the dirt.

Uncle John provided me with a small steel spring scale with a hook on it so I could weigh each chicken to determine its price.

"A two-pound chicken..." (Here he hooked the bound legs of the lowest chicken on his string and showed me how it weighed right at two pounds.) "...means you get fifty cents, and keep ten for yourself."

"Yes," I said. We shook hands on the deal.

Next day I shouldered my burden, and set off down St. Patrick Avenue. My own reluctance was small compared to that of the Rhode Island Reds, which, in their upside-down and wing-beating, squawking, vomiting and diarrheic wretchedness, provided more motivation than if Uncle John had offered me double my "commission."

Shortly after the string of chickens was in place – my own special twelve-pack of Rhode Island Reds suspended here upside down by the cotton cord cutting into the back of my neck – I myself was covered with chicken vomit and excrement.

Let me tell you, when I showed up on back door steps, the occupants were not about to invite me in. No, I was not to come one step closer. I could say my piece through the screen door. This made the sale all the more difficult.

It required much imagination to get from those creatures hung around my neck to something appetizing enough for the dinner table. Just to get them off my neck, I became the world's most motivated salesman.

"Ma'am, look at this young spring chicken. It's so young and tender its legs are smooth, not even a bump of a spur. Just feel this leg."

I'd hold out the unfortunate Red lowest on the cotton cord. At this point, the lady might open the screen door a crack and tentatively touch the leg. That was always a good sign. But it happened only once every three or four ladies.

"Yes," the lady of the house might say, withdrawing her hand behind the screen.

Encouraged, I'd go on:

"Don't you think your family would enjoy this nice tender spring chicken for dinner? If you had one now, you could have it right there on the table ready to carve by supper time."

I wanted her to imagine the chicken, slicing into it, happily passing it around to husband and children.

Silence behind the screen told me it was still a far piece from this live feathered chicken to something she wanted to put on the dinner table. So I would speak up quickly.

"How 'bout if I wring its neck and pluck the feathers, ma'am? Out by the shed, of course, so there won't be any mess to clean up."

"Yes, indeed, young man. That certainly would be nice."

Her agreement on this point meant she saw in her mind's eye the cleanly plucked chicken in her own kitchen. And if she'd gotten that far, then in her mind she'd already bought it. It was in the door, in her kitchen; it was her chicken.

"That's easy, ma'am. I'll be glad to do it right now," I'd say, then I'd head for the shed.

I charged five cents for the neck-wringing and another ten cents for the plucking, in addition to my nickel out of the two bits a pound for the chicken itself. Fair enough. Uncle John supplied the chickens; I supplied the labor.

The quicker I could dispose of my twelve-pack, the sooner I could return home, where Mother was waiting to hose me down by the outside spigot and give me fresh, clean clothes, before sending me on back to Uncle John's to pick up another string. Poor Mother, she did her part for Uncle John and Aunt Clara. She hung out so many of my clothes on the line every day, the neighbors thought she had gone to taking in other folks' wash. She rubbed her hands raw on the washboard.

After a while I got the hang of it. I was motivated by the knowledge that the sooner I got done with one string the sooner I could get into those nice, clean clothes. I could give the neck a twirl and have the cleanly plucked chicken back at the door in five minutes. For a two-pound chicken, neck wrung and plucked, she'd pay sixty-five cents, twenty-five of which was mine. I was on the road from sunrise till sunset. Each night Mother put ointment on the back of my neck.

I didn't tell Uncle John about this windfall of mine; he received the two bits a pound he'd bargained for. When I discussed the matter at Sunday dinner, Mother and Daddy agreed with me, as did Father Chambon, who began to revise his notion of my future. Daddy had seen this entrepreneurial spark in me all along. It confirmed his view: I was headed in a direction other than that of the priesthood.

The way I look at it now, those seven hundred chickens gave me an opportunity to find out something about myself that I hadn't known. If it hadn't been for Uncle John's chickens, I might not have gotten the idea of how you turn the worst sort of work into an opportunity for success.

The day I sold the last chicken, a weight was lifted from me – literally and figuratively. I had seven dollars and eighty cents in my pocket, two dollars and forty cents of which was mine. I walked back and left Uncle John's money with Aunt Clara. Mother hosed me down for the last time and gave me a fresh set of clothes. It was early August.

'The Donaldsonville Six'
vs. the big boys from Baton Rouge

Come September I was back in school at Catholic High. I was a conscientious student, but athletics was my love.

I was first string guard on Brother Hugh's championship basketball team. What a ragtag bunch we were: "Skyhook" Castanza, "Brain Trust" Thibaut, "Blond Blizzard" Waguespack, "Wild Deer" Daigle, "Old Reliable" Nereaux, and me, "Rub" Orso. Only six of us, but we played our hearts out for Brother Hugh, who, besides basketball, taught us French, algebra, religion, English literature and Latin.

A Baton Rouge crowd packed LSU's Huey Long Field House for the championship game. We'd never played for so big a crowd. And except for a lively but small contingent from Donaldsonville, made up mostly of our classmates and families, the crowd wasn't in our corner. We were in enemy territory. The Baton Rouge boys sported flashy new uniforms and sneakers.

Brother Hugh told us not to be distracted.

"Pay no mind. Just stick to the plan. Give and go. Look for the open man. Keep moving. Don't let up. Keep your eye on the goal," he said.

We did as he instructed us, and with about fifteen seconds to play in the fourth quarter, we trailed by just a point, and we had possession of the ball in our defensive court. Brother Hugh signaled for us to take our last time out. We huddled around him in front of our bench. He hunkered down with his chalk and slate. The crowd pressed in around the court, squeezing out onto it. It was bedlam.

Brother Hugh calmly diagramed a simple play we'd practiced a thousand times. Brain Trust was to be on the wing out on the right, with me out front on the left facing our offensive basket. He drew a circle where I was to be.

"Okay, now Old Reliable, you bring the ball up. Bring it up quick so they can't get too set. When you get here, Old Reliable, look at me, when you get here, on the right, pass to Brain Trust on the right wing, and go over here and set a pick for Rub on the other side."

That was my cue to go down the middle, and take the pass from Brain Trust.

"Now listen up, if this man here comes out to get you, Rub, you look to your left for Old Reliable, who's going to roll off that pick around this way and go for the basket. He's our man, unless nobody comes out to pick up Rub. You got that? Don't telegraph the pass, Rub. You hear?"

I heard. A simple play: If no one picked me up, the basket was mine. If someone did, it was up to Old Reliable. I dished the ball off to Old Reliable, who laid it up off the backboard left-handed as easy and smooth as cream. The little tick-tick of the ball touching off the backboard into the net stunned the crowd into silence. That is, all except for the fifty souls from Donaldsonville, who we could hear for the first time in the game.

Brother Hugh had pulled us through. He hadn't let us let up. He had taught us how a bunch of ragtag boys from the country with holes in their uniforms and the tread on their sneakers just about gone, who'd played most of their games in gymnasiums that looked like barns, could come out big winners in the Huey Long Field House.

But more than that, he kept us mindful of where we came from and who we were. Let me tell you, it did wonders for our self-esteem.

CHAPTER 3

Never Quit

S UCCESS DEPENDS ON MANY THINGS, BUT ONE indespensible ingredient is perseverance. To persevere, Webster says, is "to persist in an enterprise in spite of counter influences, opposition, or discouragement." My classmates and I learned perseverance from Brother Hugh.

Brother Hugh included stamina, tenacity and endurance in his idea of perseverance. These were mental as well as physical. Perseverance was a virtue planted deeply in the person you were, growing from faith in the rightness of the path you chose to follow. His lessons in the importance of perseverance were not direct, but more demonstrations in which the word "perseverance" might never be heard.

For example, that championship basketball game in Baton Rouge showed how perseverance grew from faith. Patient faith in our game plan was victory's ground work. Play your game and wait for your chance.

Basketball for Brother Hugh was not just basketball; it wasn't even mainly basketball. Mixed into it was the idea that six pretty solid guys from Donaldsonville up against teams with twelve or fifteen players could win if they had their wits about them and were ready to run and run and run.

"Mental stamina is where the games are won or lost. That goes for life in general," Brother Hugh told us.

For youngsters who had come up through the long, dark Depression years, he spoke about how we and the people we lived with lived. He put words to what our flesh and blood and bones felt. When things get hard, he'd say, when all your juices seem like they're dried up, gut it out. Do what it takes.

As you get older the meanings of words change as your body and mind change. The older you get the more physical stamina and mental stamina merge, because your body and mind become less and less distinguishable. But for boys fifteen or sixteen years old, body and mind are still ordinarily separate. Physical stamina is the easier part.

Brother Hugh demanded miles of road work on the levee, endless rope-jumping, sit-ups and push-ups, and then sprints until toward the end we couldn't tell what was physical from what was mental.

However, mental stamina was Brother Hugh's specialty. He was tough. He knew, though a young man himself, that even physical stamina in the end came down to mental stamina – mind over body. One way to acquire this mental stamina was through the discipline of repetition, of going back and back and back to whatever it was you were trying to do – whether it was learning a left-handed hook or tackling a difficult algebra problem – going back and back until you did it. Both of these endeavors, according to Brother Hugh, required mental discipline and focus.

Foreign language – Latin and French – Brother Hugh taught with mind-grinding intensity. We would think in Latin and French. The mind could control its habitual ways of thinking. Our responses to his questions told Brother Hugh whether we were thinking in French.

"Think in the language you're speaking. Your mind's ability to control itself is what success in this life is going to be all about," he'd tell us. "If your mind hasn't got a grip on itself, it won't have a grip on much else, will it?"

Yes, this made sense. In French class we thought in French and talked French till we dreamed in French. In algebra we thought in algebra, as though it was a language.

Mental stamina required the mind's control of itself, which came from continual mental exercise: hard and demanding use over an extended period. Brother Hugh conditioned the mind as he conditioned the body, by rigorously exercising it. To this concept Brother Hugh was religiously devoted.

Lord help us, when it came to concentrating all of our mental energy and capacity into a single sharp focus, Shakespeare was Brother Hugh's ultimate device. With Shakespeare's help, Brother Hugh taught us things we didn't know we were learning at the time. Now I can tell you that all my life I've been using ideas or ideas that came from ideas that Brother Hugh, without my knowing it, taught me.

In English literature class Brother Hugh had us stand and recite whole passages, pages, sometimes whole scenes and acts of Shakespeare's great dramas. We filled our minds with the minds of Shakespeare's characters till in our minds we became more than ourselves. The idea was to imagine ourselves as another person so completely that we naturally thought and spoke as that other person did. As Brother Hugh saw it, to speak Hamlet's words you had to think Hamlet's thoughts.

Today people write books about "thinking outside the box." Brother Hugh was ahead of them. Brother Hugh at once recalled to us who we were and told us to think beyond who we were, so that our notion of who we were grew.

In time and with hard and demanding use, our minds and feelings quickened with the words and thoughts of Shakespeare's characters. We learned to learn whole passages, to play out the scenes of lives other than our own, but also curiously like our own immediate Donaldsonville lives, so that our own lives grew double and triple and quadruple what they had been, just through the persistent exercise of our own inborn capacities to imagine.

There's a big chunk of imagination in perseverance. Long before the coming of the Internet, Brother Hugh opened for us a view of other worlds in which we could live beyond our physical existences.

Today people call this "virtual reality." Again, Brother Hugh got the jump on them. He showed us that even if we never managed to leave Donaldsonville, we could travel widely. We played out plays within plays within plays. Each added a layer of existence. What computers do for youngsters today, our imaginations did for us then. We learned we could do great things; if we persevered, we could achieve seemingly impossible dreams.

A simple recipe for success, for victory? Hang in there. Don't quit. Follow the plan. Win.

Yes, but success, winning, didn't often come so easily, didn't happen right away. You might have to run that play a thousand times in practice to get it to happen the way you wanted it to happen when the game was on the line. You did not enter Hamlet's mind the first time you knocked. Or the second, or the third. Success might require a circuitous route to a victory of a sort you hadn't expected. So, add patience to the list of ingredients.

The hard thing about perseverance is that you have to persevere. It wouldn't be perseverance if you didn't. The exercise of patience, in Brother Hugh's view, was a form of faith.

"You can't always know in advance what shape success will take," he once told us. "So just keep working on it. This is where the strong conviction comes in. And the success you finally achieve may not be exactly the success you had in mind when you started out. It could be even better."

Slugging it out at LSU (1940-43)

At LSU, following Brother Hugh's suggestion, I pursued degrees in journalism and English literature. Expressing myself in words, Brother

Hugh had determined from the essays I wrote under his tutelage, was my forte. He liked my style, my "word work," as he called it.

"Word work is hard work," he'd muse, looking out of the schoolroom's dusty windows. "But, Rub, it's your kind of mind's work. You enjoy it. You've got a talent for it. You know the Biblical story of the man with five talents. And for learning about life's possibilities, Rub, there's nothing like literature. Trust me."

Brother Hugh encouraged me greatly. He wrote "well done" on my compositions. I trusted Brother Hugh. He was right about my enjoyment of this kind of work. I liked writing the essays he assigned to us.

As a first semester freshman at LSU I had a problem: I was hungry all the time. Though I was a skinny kid, I had a football player's appetite. Hunger gnawed audibly in my gut as I sat in class trying to concentrate on what our professor was saying.

On the way to class that morning, I'd had my usual breakfast: my pint of milk and two diminutive banana-shaped donuts, which I ate sitting on the curb across the street from the football stadium. A nickel for the milk, a nickel for the two donuts. Most of the time, I ate the same thing for lunch and the same thing for dinner. Back in Donaldsonville, even in the Depression days, dogs had more various, and more nutritious, diets.

Well, let me tell you, I was in my own depression. Most of the money I'd saved up from my summer business enterprises had gone to purchase books, which were not, as my parents believed, provided free by Governor Huey Long, as were books in high school.

So day after day in the hot September and October sun, I ate my monotonous meals on the hard curbstones across the street from the football stadium. Try as I might, even with my eyes closed tight, I could not transmute a banana-shaped donut into a beefsteak. Once it hit the tongue, all illusion dissolved in my own saliva.

Football players in my classes talked about the "training table." If they were on a scholarship, they got to eat at the training table with the other scholarship athletes, where they feasted on steaks, vegetables and fresh fruit.

"E.J.," one football player classmate would say, "sometimes, after dinner, I'm so stuffed I can't move. One of these nights they're going to have to carry me out on a stretcher."

At this point in his narrative, my beefy informant would slap his belly. I made it a rule to avoid the subject of food with these well-fed classmates.

On the curb with my milk and donuts, I ate with my head down, sucking the milk through a straw to wash the dry donuts down my throat, hoping the athletes coming and going from their big meals across the street didn't notice me. I couldn't help but see them as they came out, slapping their stuffed guts, loosening their belts.

My belt? In the first notch it was already loose. My self-esteem crouched right down there with me on the curb.

At night, I dreamed I saw the training table loaded, bowing under the weight of the piles of thick, rare steaks and collards, corn, string beans and potatoes. Oh, man. All the beefy, overstuffed football players sat at their places reaching for the platters of food, shoveling it in, their jaws working hard. My hunger-burdened imagination groaned under the food's great weight. My dream never showed me there with the chosen ones.

But the training table was no picnic table like those we sat at to eat the crawfish and boiled corn and spicy potatoes back home, where you didn't need an invitation at all, where there was a place for everybody. No, the training table was a kind of very exclusive club, like the one in Donaldsonville where the wealthy widows went to play *bourrée*. You had to be a member; you had to have an athletic scholarship in football, basketball, boxing, track or baseball.

I did have a scholarship, awarded for my academic accomplishments at Catholic High of Donaldsonville, where I had delivered the class of 1940's salutary oration. I would have preferred an athletic scholarship, which included books and food. It appeared the university did not consider meals as important to academic as to athletic achievement.

But, at LSU's level of competition, I was too small for football and too short for basketball. So, what was a hungry 135-pound journalism student to do? What would I have to do to earn a place at the training table?

The answer – what I thought was the answer – appeared, magically, early one morning. *The Reveille* I picked up on the way to class had a photo of Roy Amedee, an amateur boxer of considerable accomplishment, who that fall had enrolled as a freshman at LSU. A lightweight, 133 pounds, he looked like an ordinary skinny freshman. He stood in the boxer's crouch, gloves at the ready, dark eyes focused on an opponent not shown.

Way back in Sisters of Charity grammar school, I'd done my share of school yard fighting. We squared off on the hard-packed dirt and fought with our fists till the sister came out to break it up or one of the combatants gave in. In fact, we didn't so much fight as box, in the manner of "Gentleman Jim" Corbett.

There were rules, a sort of code of honor, which you stuck to, even if you were being beaten. You didn't hit someone who was down. You didn't kick or bite or choke. You boxed. The objective was to bloody your opponent's nose, to blacken his eyes, to out-box him. Beat him by the rules. The winner was the one who was left standing.

The code of the boxer, which placed much emphasis upon endurance, appealed to me. I had been schooled in endurance. The fighter who endured won.

Among our boyhood models, all of whom we got to see in the newsreels that preceded the features at the Grand Theatre, Henry Armstrong was my favorite. Little "Hammering Henry" Armstrong, also known as "Hurricane" Armstrong. I never forgot the newsreel showing Armstrong – a lightweight, weighing no more than 133 pounds – hammering the bigger and more experienced Barney Ross for fifteen rounds in New York's Madison Square Garden. What a fight. I must have watched that newsreel a dozen times.

Talk about endurance and stamina and tenacity. "Hammering Henry" went on to win one hundred and fifty fights, one hundred by knock out. He had tenacity in spades. Fighters just don't last that long anymore.

Henry Armstrong was someone with whom I identified. A fighter my size. I committed to memory his every move in that newsreel fight: the look on his face when he jabbed, when he threw a right hook, when he sat in his corner listening to his trainer, when he was moving in for the kill. I thought I could think his thoughts.

So when I got back from class that day, I tried a few jabs, a couple of hooks before the cloudy mirror in my dorm room. I tried on Henry Armstrong's looks. After a semester of milk and donuts, I was ready to fight. Boxing was my meal ticket. I raised my arms in victory.

A cagey Lebanese named Ed Khoury coached the LSU boxing team, which under his direction had become the perennial National Collegiate Athletic Association (NCAA) boxing champion. During Khoury's reign, boxing was king at LSU. There was great honor in being a member of the LSU boxing team.

I reported to the fieldhouse, gloved, ready for action. Coach Khoury, whose throne consisted of a high stool in the center of the gymnasium, took my name and flicked his cagey black eyes over me, taking in what I hoped appeared like a future Henry Armstrong. Out of the corner of my eye I recognized Roy Amedee jumping rope.

The gym was full of fighters, working on the punching bags, sparring, jumping rope. They were all shapes and sizes – heavyweights, middleweights, flyweights, and lightweights like myself and Henry Armstrong. At the far end a makeshift ring had been set up on the wooden gym floor. A match was in progress; a couple of heavyweights were going at it tooth and nail. My heart raced. I was hoping he'd send me down to the ring, to show him my stuff.

Instead, with a small movement of his head, a sort of boxer's feint, he directed my eye to a corner of the gym that was occupied by the heavy punching bags. Coach Khoury, a man of few words, demonstrated a one-two, one-two punching motion with his hands, barely stirring on his throne. One of the heavy bags was not in use, as if it had been expecting me. Its large bruised label introduced it: Everlast – pounded, I fancied, by generations of LSU's NCAA champions.

Okay, Mr. Everlast. I squared up in front of the bag, and proceeded to hammer — one-two, one-two, one-two. Mr. Everlast took it all, everything I had to dish out. One-two, one-two. In a short while, the muscles in my arms swelled up and got as heavy as chunks of old scrap iron in a Donaldsonville shed. My punches slowed and slowed. One ... two ... one ... two. I felt like I was swimming in an ocean of mud.

"How you like Mr. Everlast, hey?" Coach Khoury barked out.

I hung on to the vision of the training table with the T-bones and kept punching.

"You like Mr. Everlast?"

I kept punching. *Hammering Henry*, I thought. *Hammering Henry Armstrong.* Finally, Coach Khoury must have liked what he saw, because he said, okay, I could be on the practice squad. *Okay*, I thought.

Things don't always turn out the way you've imagined them. My epithet became not "Hammering Henry" but, as I said earlier, "Hamburger Ourso."

My nemesis turned out to be the very same Roy Amedee, whose photo I'd seen in the *Reveille* that fall morning. He wasn't in the *Reveille* for nothing. At 133 pounds, Roy Amedee had not lost a fight in the eight years he had been fighting as an amateur. He was expected to be the NCAA lightweight champion his first year on the squad.

In the gym his hands moved far quicker than the eye. Quicker than my eye, anyway. He had no intention of relinquishing his spot on the team to a no-account, starving walk-on from Donaldsonville. Roy Amedee fought with cold, calculating, intense fury, hard to imagine from that *Reveille* photo. The scholarship lightweight, he stood squarely in my path to the athletes' training table.

Oh, Coach Khoury gave me plenty of encouragement.

"Get up Ourso and knock the sonofabitch out," he'd say.

This only infuriated the swift and crafty Roy Amedee. He danced in and out, right and left, flashing straight left jabs, right hooks, punches I never saw till they hit their target – usually my nose, or jaw. Roy Amedee was precise, fast, and elusive.

He was always just beyond reach. I plodded around the ring after him. He threw punches like a hurricane. Bang, bang-bang-bang, bang-bang. To the body, then to the head. He'd long ago picked up on Henry Armstrong. The coaches called him Roy "Hurricane" Amedee. His combinations bloodied my face, my gut ached, my eyes swelled, my nose ran red, until I resembled the piece of red meat I craved. The taste in my mouth was my own salty blood. That's when Coach Khoury dubbed me "Hamburger Ourso."

"Hamburger, get up, get up and knock the sonofabitch out," he said.

I never stayed down. I got up. I got knocked down again. For Roy Amedee, NCAA Intercollegiate Champion, I was maybe a sort of technologically advanced punching bag – one that moved, threw punches, got up when you knocked it down, and kept trying but couldn't knock you down.

I was too hungry to quit – which Coach Khoury knew when he put me on the practice squad.

In three years I never missed a practice. But I never won a fight. Hell, I never won a round. Roy Amedee got his purple and gold LSU letter jacket with leather sleeves his first year. All I ever got was my own bloody shirt.

When I asked Coach Khoury whether three years of bleeding for LSU on the practice squad didn't earn me one of those purple and gold LSU jackets, he did his little feint in the direction of the gym's heavy bag corner. Did I see the Everlast with one of those jackets?

"I give you one of the letter jackets, people are going to think L is for loser," coach said to me.

This hurt like hell. More than any of the beatings I'd endured at the hands of Roy Amedee. It was a hard, hard, punishing lesson in the relation between perseverance and winning.

Though I didn't appreciate it then, Coach Khoury taught me a lesson well worth learning for the long haul, which is really where perseverance prevails. Without intending it, I formed a habit of long-haul perseverance, which I can tell you has stood me in good stead.

Merely getting up after getting knocked down repeatedly doesn't always lead directly or immediately to victory. Still, the most difficult, and important, successes in life are impossible unless we get up after getting knocked down. If you quit, you can't win. So, you've got to be a long-hauler.

Though times were lean in the food department when I first got to LSU, I don't want to give the impression that I starved for all three and a half years with no variation of diet. My hunger was assuaged in a way I hadn't at all anticipated. My salvation in this department came about not from my pugilistic but from my verbal dexterity. Brother Hugh's observation about my mind's bent for "word work" proved to be more accurate than I imagined.

To be sure, I hungered for the delights of the training table but also, just as much, for enlightenment, for knowledge. I wanted to know. And it was that second kind of hunger that in its own roundabout way led to the satisfaction not only of itself but also of the hunger that so insistently gnawed at my gut.

Without any money to spend running around, I read and read and read. I read chemistry, biology and American and European history, as well as literature, sociology and political science. I read the chapters we were assigned and then I went to the library and read the suggested readings at the end of the chapters. So, when I got to class, I was overprepared. Of course, this pleased my professors.

LSU enlarged my view of how much there really was to know. I wasn't more than thirty or forty miles from Donaldsonville, but I felt the hugeness of the world all around me. I was in a state of continual excitement.

As for my physical hunger, Providence smiled on me. At LSU, as I've said, I was a journalism and English literature major and so, with my background in athletics, naturally I reported sports for *The Reveille* and, during summers, for the *Morning Advocate*.

The City Editor on the *Advocate*, Maggie Dixon, took me under her wing. We were both from Ascension Parish, and I guess she took it upon herself to look out for this hungry Donaldsonville boy. She took every opportunity to assign me to events connected with food – dinners, banquets, breakfasts, always making sure that I would be fed. She didn't care that the other reporters grew suspicious. She'd just give the assignment:

"E.J., I want you to cover the All Star Athletic Banquet. They eat at six. Get there around five forty-five."

That meant I'd get a plate of whatever it was they were eating. It wasn't the training table, but it put some dietary variety in my life and kept some meat on my bones. Without this bit of Divine Providence I would have had to exist on milk and donuts for three and a half years. I don't want to imagine what that would have been like.

Off to war (1943-46)

The war, as I've said, interrupted my days at LSU, cutting short both my academic and athletic pursuits, and thrusting me headlong into my generation's great conflict. The gentlemanly code of the boxing ring didn't hold where I was headed. These were, as they say, the times that try men's souls, mine along with the rest.

For those of us who were of fighting age there were very few exemptions. In the middle of my senior year at LSU, my Reserve Officer Training Corps (ROTC) unit was called up. We were eager recruits.

Roy Amedee and the rest of us said good-bye to Coach Khoury. We left him alone and for once bewildered, perched on his throne in the empty gym, so suddenly silent he could hear his own breathing.

I went home to say good-bye to my parents and brother and sister. Now that the U.S.A. was in it, all our attention and energy focused on the war. Suddenly life's preoccupations up to that point became inconsequential. Everything hinged upon victory. Everybody in Donaldsonville forty and younger it seemed was off to the war. I was proud to be a part of my country's effort.

I said good-bye to Margy, to whom I'd begun to write regular letters. We sat together at T. Royal's Restaurant for a long, lazy Sunday afternoon in January. Her green eyes were watery. She made me promise to keep on writing. She hadn't yet met Frank Heard. Her smile, all her expressions, her green eyes, and her beautiful hair, beginning to be just perceptibly streaked with the premature silver characteristic of her family – these became fixed in all their detail and color in my mind. I couldn't have made it through the war without that.

On Monday I got on a crowded Greyhound headed for Officers Candidate School. Donaldsonville dwindled behind us and was gone in a hot swirl of road dust. The Greyhound bounced over the potholes and out on to the River Road headed for the military base at Alexandria.

The Army commissioned me as a second lieutenant and sent me to Fort Sill in Lawton, Oklahoma, where I taught new recruits to assemble and disassemble machine guns. They had to know all the parts by name and to be able to take them apart and put them back together blindfolded. Then I was assigned to the Mule Pack Artillery Unit slated for special training maneuvers in the mountains around Colorado Springs, Colorado.

In the days of the war when it was anticipated that the invasion of Europe would be undertaken from Norway, it had been decided that the Mule Pack was to haul artillery that would support the front line troops. Lucky me. I was an artillery officer. We needed to learn how to manage our field pieces and the mules in mountains, and in snow.

While in mountainous Colorado, we Mule Packers slept in tents or often just in sleeping bags. It was freezing, and it snowed every day. Lord help us, we never got to stand on level ground out there.

Everything we did we did in this terrible cold. Like the mules themselves, we officers and men never got to go indoors. If I had visions of food back at LSU, in Colorado I had visions of heated interiors, warm rooms with horizontal floors and steam radiators gurgling all night. At night, freezing in my sleeping bag, I tried to imagine that my boots and clothes were dry and warm.

Was there something in my genetic background that doomed me always to be on the outside looking in - at beefy football players feasting on steaks, at warm people at ease around a blazing fireplace? Let me tell you, three months of training in Colorado, from December into March, took an awful lot of perseverance.

There was wind and blizzards. Ice storms. The snow drifted up around our tents till we couldn't tell a tent from a mound of snow. The Army mules stood rear end to the wind, blinking, blinking, uncomplaining, ears twitching, shooting white clouds of breath from wide nostrils. I tried to think like a mule, hoping thereby to gain some of their patient endurance. This mental exercise did not enhance my self-esteem. Nor did it keep me warm.

To handle mules, the Army said you had to be at least a certain height, because that height was necessary to properly balance the pack on a mule's back. The mules carried in "cradles" on their backs the eight pieces of our French 75mm guns. You want an unbalanced mule on your string on a narrow mountain trail?

Now, rather than take the time to measure each candidate, the Army ingeniously devised a quick measure that at once assessed our physical and mental qualifications for the job. The officer in charge told us to run under a wood beam that was set at the minimum height. Those who ducked were tall enough for the Mule Pack.

Standing in the line, waiting my turn, I saw what was happening. I took stock. I certainly hadn't aspired to the Mule Pack. *Don't duck, Ous.* It turned out the beam was set at precisely six feet. Of course, I hit my head. When I got up from the mud the officer informed me I had passed with flying colors.

"You're in the Mule Pack, Mr. Ourso," he said. "Tall enough and dumb enough – too dumb to duck. Congratulations."

"Yes, sir. Thank you," I said, still a little wobbly.

He returned my salute with a grin. And that was it.

Again my self-esteem plummeted down, down, down. Oh, if I'd only been just a couple of inches shorter, I'd have been in Georgia or some other warmer, more level place.

But let me tell you, hard-headedness, perseverance, endurance were exactly what was needed out there in Camp Carson, Colorado. The encampment was huge – thousands of men, trucks, guns, and more mules than I'd dreamed existed. This was really my first close encounter with mules, having seen only the few plow mules that Grandpa Falcon kept on his farm. My grandfather's mules, hitched to a plow, would pull when asked, most of the time. But these Missouri mules didn't take orders well at all. They had to be shown. Even then they resisted. Maybe they knew what was ahead; maybe they knew something we didn't. Most of the time, they didn't cooperate; we had to pull them.

In the Army I learned mule pack perseverance, not only as it applied to mules but mainly as it applied to human beings. Mule pack perseverance keeps you moving forward on and on, over any sort of terrain, uphill and downhill in the face of freezing cold, steadily, undistracted, not hurrying, but never stopping either.

In the Mule Pack, the mule was a privileged creature, a sort of prince; we officers and men were the mule's slaves. Nobody rode a mule – except for the General, the Division Commander. Yes, the mules had to carry the heavy cradles laden with the disassembled French 75s. We didn't envy them that.

But we officers and men had to clear the way for the mules, with brush hooks and shovels and axes. There were no trails where we went. We fought for every foot of forward progress. Up mountainsides thick with snow-laden aspen saplings, we had to chop a way for the mules. Over terrain where the snow had drifted to shoulder height, we had to shovel a path for the mules. We might be out in the freezing snow and wind and sleet for days, plodding forward, beating a trail for the lordly Missouri mules.

Whew! We worked up a hell of a sweat. Everybody sweated, officers included. No self-respecting officer would stand there and watch his men do the work. We worked alongside the men. Drenched in sweat, when we stopped for lunch or supper, our wet underwear would freeze stiff if we didn't keep moving.

As for Lord Mule, at the end of each day's trek he had to be brushed until he was dry. We couldn't turn in before that was done.

Finally, we squirmed into our sleeping bags fully clothed, just our noses sticking out, so beat-down tired that we slept despite our cold, wet clothes. In the morning we woke covered with new snow. We ate our cold K-ration breakfast and went on. Miraculously, nobody caught cold or got sick, except for frostbite.

I wrote to Margy describing my tribulations, leaving out, however, the details of the qualifying examination. She must have discerned in my tone disappointment and chagrin at being placed in so lowly a station. Margy always knew what I was thinking as well as I did myself. She wrote back that it was nothing to be ashamed of, that it was "good, honest duty on behalf of our country." I should get my chin up, because it's never a disgrace to serve, no matter how humble the service.

"And get that hangdog look off your face," she admonished me. "I know you. I know it's there. Just think of how much higher you're going to climb."

Margy's always been one to pick me up when I was down.

Once I wrote to Margy about the snow.

"A winter wonderland," I joked. "In the meadow there's a snow mule."

She thought that was a healthier attitude to take. Her return letter's light, bantering, friend-to-friend tone was nevertheless somehow troubling. Nothing I could put my finger on, but not what I wanted. Had she met someone?

I hung tough and sent off another letter of a more serious tone.

When you're in the Army, your home battles are fought at great disadvantage. You're not there. I knew nothing about the dentist from New Orleans.

While I was in Colorado the U.S.'s overall military strategy changed. Norway dropped out of the picture. The Army shipped the mules back to Missouri. I envied them. Our artillery unit was to be motorized. We packed up the artillery – the Long Toms, the 105s, the 75s – and left Colorado, late in the spring of 1944. In a convoy of deuce-and-a-halfs, we headed for training at Fort Benning, Georgia, where it was now summer.

Ironically, comfortable as it was, in the steamy warmth of Georgia, it seemed that everyone soon had a cold, or pleurisy, or the flu, or even, in some cases, pneumonia. I escaped with a bout of the common cold.

At Fort Benning the entire division underwent massive retraining in the use of all sorts of trucks and armored vehicles. But it turned out that the training we received in the operation of the machines and transport of the big guns was less critical to our ultimate mission than was our training in Colorado's snow and freezing cold.

After a summer and fall of training, we landed in France, made our way southeast to Nancy and on through Alsace-Lorraine to join General Patton's 3rd Army. We were just in time for Patton's forty-eight hour Christmas express run from Verdun, France, to Bastogne, Belgium, to cut the German supply routes from the east and to rescue General A.C. McAuliffe's famous 101st Airborne Division, by then completely surrounded by a massive German counteroffensive.

We were fresh replacements for men who had been fighting in France since D-Day, June 6. For us, now members of the 4th Armored Division, the war was to be the Battle of the Bulge, one of the biggest and most crucial encounters of the entire European campaign of 1944. Our part in it took place not in mountains but in knee-deep mud and snow, fog and sleet. The training in Colorado was on target.

At Verdun, in the cold, damp squad room in his barracks, when Eisenhower asked Patton how long it would take him to turn his 3rd Army around from facing east toward Germany to facing north toward Bastogne and the imperiled 101st Airborne, Patton replied that with proper authority and enough gasoline he could be on the outskirts of Bastogne ready to attack in forty-eight hours.

The other generals laughed.

But Patton, anticipating the need for such a daring mission, had already prepared not just one but three plans, so all he had to do to set things in motion was transmit to his subordinate officers one of three codes. He alone was prepared for exactly that meeting in the Verdun squad room. Patton would have the last laugh. Eisenhower granted his request over the other generals' objections.

Patton's 3rd Army convoy stretched out for miles and miles through the snow-filled forests and farm country of northern France: deuce-and-a-halfs, filled with men, pulling 105s, the Long Toms mounted on tractors, whose treads – and those of Lieutenant Colonel Creighton Abrams' tanks – chewed the soft roads into mush as we went. The officers were in the one-tons that rolled through the hub-high muck.

We stopped only to refuel and relieve ourselves and then sped on, eating and sleeping as best we could in the trucks. On and on and on, passing west of Luxembourg into the lovely, dark Ardennes in southeastern Belgium, where the forests thickened around us as the sounds of the massive German artillery barrage on Bastogne grew from the barely audible shadow of sound to a terrible surround-sound thundering.

Patton's orders were "drive like hell."

"It's root hog or die," Patton shouted. "Shoot the works."

I was the Executive Officer in charge of four Long Toms, the big 155s mounted on the tank-like carriers. My artillery unit set up in an open rubble-filled field just a few kilometers south of the German line surrounding Bastogne. We shelled the Germans for eighteen hours straight, without letup, without any respite after our long drive north. Smoke and fog hung in the broken and torn limbs of the trees of the woods that surrounded us. Our orders were to keep firing until the German line was broken.

The Germans proved to be much tougher than we had anticipated.

By all estimations except General Eisenhower's, they were an exhausted force, incapable of the counteroffensive they had mounted. But it was their last gasp.

The day after Christmas of 1944, the 37th Tank Battalion, with its twenty Shermans under the command of Lieutenant Colonel Creighton Abrams, drove through the German line, breaking the siege of Bastogne. Just ahead of the tanks, P-47s had hit the village in Abrams' path on their last bombing run. Abrams pushed on without stopping. When the first vehicles of the 4th Armored Division crossed the lines of the 101st Airborne, General McAuliffe, who had held out for eleven days under intense bombardment, was greatly relieved, to put it mildly.

"Gee, I am mighty glad to see you," he said.

It has been said that for those of us who played a part in the rescue of the 101st Airborne at Bastogne, this was the defining moment of our lives. It was a unique moment of never-to-be-forgotten victory granted after indescribable effort, with the eventual shape of cold-war Europe hanging in the balance – a moment impossible to duplicate, or even to fully comprehend. Had Hitler succeeded at Bastogne, he would have had clear sailing to Antwerp – and the war would have gone on longer than it did, thus costing both sides many more lives before it ended.

Selling insurance

At thirty, I had a wonderful wife and five handsome babies; I had my own funeral home and burial insurance business; we lived in a spacious house. But not on Easy Street.

I did night-shift baby feeding and diaper and bottle washing; I was back-up ambulance driver and door-to-door salesman of burial insurance. My shoe soles wore out. Dark circles appeared under my eyes. Payrolls haunted my dreams. Margy kept me going.

"Ous, we're going to make it," she'd say frequently.

Mornings I talked to myself in the mirror:

Hamburger, get up and knock the sonofabitch out. Keep firing till we break through the lines. Don't quit.

Words were my stock-in-trade; selling more burial insurance than anybody in Louisiana was my goal; five hungry babies were my motivation.

Ous, I said each morning to the face in the mirror, *get out there and sell like you've never sold before.*

At a nickel a stop I had miles to go before I slept. Competitors sabotaged my hours of hard work. When I found my policies impaled on picket fences, my spirits fell. I prayed for perseverance in all its various forms.

Lord help me, I prayed. *Don't let me quit.*

Selling insurance policies is not like selling live chickens. The live chicken you hold out for viewing. If you have to, you can sell it through a dusty screen door. Wring its neck and pluck it and hand it over. A hand reaches out with the money, takes hold of the chicken.

With insurance you are selling something people can't see. Insurance is intangible. You are selling peace of mind, reassurance. It can't be sold through a screen door. You have to give it life in words, in language your customer will understand.

So, go 'round to the back door, especially if it's a house with a manicured front yard, and knock. Stand where the woman of the house can see you through the screen door. Talk to the woman, because she's the one who's worrying she's going to be left to make funeral arrangements.

You hope she'll ask you in and offer you a cool drink. The best place to do your selling is at the kitchen table.

"Ma'am, I'm E.J. Ourso," I'd say, holding out my business card for her inspection. "Remember me? The kid who used to collect scrap newspaper and iron. I cleaned out that old shed in your yard."

"Yes, E.J. Didn't you sell spring chickens one summer?"

"Yes, ma'am, I did. And strings of garlic, too."

"Well, look at you, E.J. How time flies."

"Yes, I'm married with five children of my own."

Reassured, she'll invite me in, set a cool drink on the table. We'll talk about the war, and the boys who have come home, and some who didn't. About Armistice Day. Seems that the women are always sympathetic with a veteran, though it is difficult for them to imagine war. The mud, racket, pervasiveness of death.

Getting to the subject of burial insurance is not easy. Burial is not a pleasant subject for conversation among the living.

I don't hurry. I sip my cool lemonade, look about the kitchen at the old chairs, the scarred table, the worn linoleum on the floor, the fly-speckled ceiling, the ceiling fan turning slowly overhead. By now the woman has read my card and knows why I'm there.

My message is fundamental: It's not *if*; it's *when*. I explain what burial insurance will do for her, describing the elegant furniture and cool corridors of the funeral home that will provide services when they are needed.

"There's a coffee room for guests. We make all the arrangements just as you want them made. It's air conditioned. We just put down new carpet. Peaceful green. This insurance will set your mind at ease."

I conjure up for her the solid benefits represented by the words and numbers on the piece of paper, lying flat on her kitchen table between us. I must make this peace of mind as real to her as the table itself, all with words, words.

And just at the right time, when I can see that she understands what I am talking about, I talk numbers. You have to know exactly when to talk about numbers, because numbers are even more abstract than words, and at the same time frightening to one unaccustomed to talking about numbers and burial.

"You pay just a nickel a week. A nickel a week buys you peace of mind.

You can go on about your business."

A nickel a week. Who that lived in a house, with a backyard and an overhead fan in the kitchen and an icebox and a stove, who had a husband with a solid job at a nearby plant, and all those kids peeping at me around the corner, who in such circumstances of life didn't have a nickel a week to assure peace of mind?

She had to see at once how insignificant and in the long haul how significant this nickel could be. For peace of mind. For knowing that when that hard time came, she would have what she needed. Whatever the substantial benefits of burial insurance were, and believe me, when needed they are substantial, at the rate of a nickel a week it had to seem like she was getting something for practically nothing.

That was my approach.

Of course, each client had her own questions and misgivings, required her own explanations. Could a nickel a week possibly pay such expenses as those of a funeral in so well-furnished and -appointed a funeral home?

Funerals are something with which every adult has had at least some experience. We know caskets, burial plots and flowers must be purchased, regardless of whether we are ready to undertake such expenses. These expenses cannot be put off. We must meet them somehow. A woman who does not work outside the home, who finds herself suddenly without her husband's income, is in difficult straits.

My clients were white, black, French, Italian, Spanish. Most were Catholic. Many of my Cajun clients spoke only French, so I had to be able to think in French, as Brother Hugh used to say. If my client was black or Italian or Spanish, the roles changed, the talk changed. I carefully wrote down the numbers. Numbers are always the same; numbers are universal language.

The idea of insurance is not indigenous to these cultures. It requires explanation, much explanation. Death, burial – we in the midst of life think these to be so far off as to be inconsiderable, except that we know they are inevitable for all of us. My client at the table with me already knows this, not in thought but in bones and flesh. Dark, interior knowledge we share at this table.

I persevere in the sales presentation with patient and careful explanations upon explanations, with long mid-morning and afternoon kitchen table talks. We talk about what will be *when*, not *if*. I never say death. No need to.

I build the business client by client, nickel by nickel, dollar by dollar, but under all that word by word, sentence by sentence.

After making the sale and getting the contract signed, I step back into the heat and the smell of sun-scorched grass, the screen door banging shut behind me, squinting as my pupils contract in the glare.

In heat so heavy it's hard to draw a breath, I cross the street and approach the next house, hoping for a cool seat at the kitchen table, a fresh glass of lemonade, another sale that will help to feed my children.

In 1939, at age 16,
I was a high school
student at Catholic
High in Donaldsonville.

— Photography by Olan Mills

— Photo courtesy of The Donaldsonville Chief

Catholic High of Donaldsonville's 1939 basketball team won the district championship with only six players – an accomplishment which The Donaldsonville Chief *described as "an amazing feat." Standing (from left to right): Charest "Brain Trust" Thibaut, Albert "Skyhook" Castanza, Brother Hugh (coach), Mike "Blond Blizzard" Waguespack, and O.J. "Wild Deer" Daigle. Kneeling and sitting (from left): E.J. "Rub" Ourso, Arthur "Lead Ball" Montero (manager), and J.D. "Old Reliable" Nereaux.*

I don't recall what the occasion was to wear a tuxedo, but I did so in 1941 at age 18 while attending LSU. It must have been before I joined the boxing team and received regular beatings from teammate Roy Amedee!

In July of 1942, at age 19, I was a member of the staff of The Daily Reveille *at LSU in Baton Rouge. At the time I was in hot pursuit of a degree in journalism, hoping to make a living as a sports reporter. Then I got a call from Uncle Sam.*

My country called and I went to war along with thousands of other young men who were attending LSU in the early 1940s. This picture was taken in 1945. I ultimately achieved the rank of Captain in the U.S. Army and served in an artillery unit that was instrumental in the Allied victory in the Battle of the Bulge. It was an honor to serve under Gen. George Patton, a man whose example helped teach me to dream impossible dreams.

Fr. Philip Hannan was nicknamed "The Jumping Padre" because he was chaplain for the 82nd Airborne Division. We met in Belgium during World War II in 1944. He had me round up fellow soldiers for a special Mass following the Battle of the Bulge. Fr. Hannan went on to become the Archbishop of the Archdiocese of New Orleans, Louisiana.

The happiest day of my life – October 9, 1947–
was the day Margy and I became husband and wife.

E.J. and Margy Ourso, 1986

For many years the main office of Security Industrial Insurance Co.
was at 110 Railroad Ave., Donaldsonville, La.

I finally received a degree from LSU – an honorary Doctor of Humane Letters – in 1996. Making the presentation is Chancellor William Davis; next to him is Tom Clark, Dean of the Business School; the gentleman behind me is Jack Hamilton, head of the Journalism School. That same year the LSU Business School was re-named the E.J. Ourso College of Business Administration.

E.J. Ourso, 1995

– Photography by Marie Constantin, Constantin Photography, Baton Rouge, La.

CHAPTER 4

A Donaldsonville Education

I N 1970 I BECAME A MEMBER OF THE YOUNG Presidents Organization (YPO). That year I attended the week-long seminar the Harvard Business School faculty put on for the YPO each January.

To be a YPO member you had to have become president of your own company with at least 100 employees and revenues of at least $1 million before you reached 40. When I was accepted I felt as though I had at last made it to the training table.

Here I was at Harvard, sitting at the dinner table discussing business strategy with presidents of world-renowned companies that manufactured computer chips and owned supermarket chains. The president of BIC pens was a seminar participant. I had never beaten Roy Amedee at boxing, but I had a seat at the training table anyway. My self-esteem took wing.

Still, my Donaldsonville roots drew the attention of my fellow YPOers. My differences stood out. When the group chose a few members to address the current class of Harvard MBA students, I was greatly disappointed: I wasn't among the chosen few.

"Ous," they said, "we know you can speak French. What you speak best is Cajun. But these people won't understand a word you're saying."

This knocked me down because my mind was filled to bursting with things I wanted to tell these MBA students. I wanted to inspire these young people to go out and make it their way. I myself had been inspired by the life story of the great Italian entrepreneur A.P. Giannini. I just wanted an opportunity.

My door of opportunity opened unexpectedly, just a crack. One of the guys who was to speak that night didn't know the way to the auditorium, so our group's faculty advisor asked me to escort him. This humble assignment didn't do a thing to enhance my self-esteem, but I said I would take the man to the auditorium, so I did. I led him up to the stage where the other speakers were already gathered with the dean of the Harvard Business School.

Oh, I wanted to be one of the speakers in the worst way. I thought, *If you want to be a speaker, you've got to charm the person in charge.* I went up to the dean.

"Dean," I said, "I'm E.J. Ourso. I've never met a dean. Could I shake your hand?"

The dean extended his hand.

"Mr. Ourso, I'm glad you're going to be speaking tonight because I've never heard someone who sells burial insurance. I'm interested in what you have to say," he responded.

I guess he had read about me in the booklet they printed on seminar participants – the name of our company, what business we were in, where we lived, where we went to school, and so on. I pushed my door of opportunity wide open and took a big stride in.

"Oh no, dean, I'm not one of the speakers," I stated.

"Don't worry about that, Mr. Ourso. I'm the dean. I can arrange that. You just take a seat on stage," he said.

I was, after all, to be one of the speakers.

"Dean," I said, "thank you. I'd love to be one of the speakers. I'm an ex-chicken salesman. I sell burial insurance door to door."

His face lit up. This wasn't by the business school book.

"That's interesting," he said.

He wanted to know how big Donaldsonville was. Exactly where in Louisiana was it?

Burial insurance is not a flashy business, not alongside the glitz of computer chips and millions of yellow BIC pens, but I had some ideas that might help these young people launch their careers, and I burned to squeeze it all in to the half hour I was allotted. I joined the other speakers on stage. The auditorium was filling.

There were fifty YPO members there that January. Snow covered the Harvard campus, beautiful as a Christmas card. What a pleasure snow can be when it isn't connected with war. At Harvard I got to come into warm rooms in old university halls and cozy dormitories. We didn't sleep in cold sleeping bags. There were no mules. The paths were clear and dry.

In the dining hall they served us *filet mignon* with squash, string beans, and mashed potatoes with brown gravy and, after dinner, whisky sours in the lounge. Better than the training table of my dreams.

The seminars, conducted by Harvard professors, were a great chance to learn how other business people had made their way. All fifty of us had something to teach, as well as to learn. Successful people want to say, "Look, here's how I did it." There's always someone who has something to say that can help you out. Truly successful people do not need to guard the secrets of success. As I see it, opportunity's doors are opening all over the place. But you've got to step over the threshold.

Each day in the classrooms, we broke into small discussion groups to talk about cases: What would you do if you were President of XYZ Company? The previous evening each small group had met after dinner to prepare. The cocktails loosened up our tongues a little.

These heady sessions could last till midnight. Everybody had something interesting to say. Discussion was enriched by all the points of view represented by the YPO members – manufacturers of knitting needles, of computers, of computer chips; the owners of supermarkets and department stores; the president of BIC pens; guys in real estate, insurance. The next day we presented our ideas to the Harvard faculty. Discussion was enhanced by the presence of such notables as U.S. Senator Daniel Patrick Moynihan and Nobel Prize-winning economist Milton Friedman. The air sparkled with fresh ideas. Thoughts jumped among us like electricity.

Addressing Harvard business students

The night of my first presentation to the Harvard MBA students I took my place on stage with the other speakers. This ex-chicken salesman, ex-mule packer was chomping at the bit, raring to go. The dean had told the five other speakers I'd be joining them. They didn't look pleased, but what could they do? He was the dean.

"Ourso's speaking. You fellows decide the best order," he said.

They huddled to debate what to do with me. What was to be my spot in the line-up?

"I'll lead off," I volunteered.

"No, that won't work. Ous, these people speak English; you speak Cajun. We don't want you to clear the hall."

"Well, okay, I'll speak last," I volunteered, not wanting to be difficult.

No, not there either. They wanted to end on a high note.

My warm feeling of belonging began to cool down. But, okay, they decided, I'd bat in the middle of the order, after the computer chips man (a Stanford MBA) and the guy from BIC pens (a Wharton MBA). Fine.

The Stanford MBA told them all about his computer chip. Remember, this was when computers were new. His computer chip, made of acrylic, was as thin as a piece of Wrigley's chewing gum. What a marvel.

Then BIC pens talked. He declared proudly that he was a graduate from the best MBA program in the country, and he went on and on about the great education he had received and so forth, and then he told them he was a Wharton MBA. The audience fell silent. They were thinking, *Boo. Get out of here; go back to Philadelphia.*

My turn.

I strode to the podium and grasped it as if to assault it. In the silence that followed my predecessor from Wharton, I had their attention.

"My name is Ous Ourso," I said. "I don't have an MBA from Wharton. Don't even have a college degree. I left college because General Patton needed me at Bastogne. Never had an economics course, or a business course. I got my education in Donaldsonville, Louisiana, where I sell burial insurance. I own funeral homes and burial insurance companies. We insure the service we provide. I may not be smart. But I'm rich."

They cheered.

I took a nickel and a dollar out of my pocket and held them up over my head.

"A nickel a stop, twenty stops to the dollar," I bellowed.

I explained how I did that, how I talked to the women at the kitchen tables till peace of mind was something they could reach out and touch, how I wore holes in my shoes so that I had to empty out the road dirt before Margy would let me in the door.

Of course, I told them how I couldn't have made it without Margy. My wife and children were powerful motivators. I told them what the years had taught me: There are all sorts of paths to success – intelligence, credentials, like MBAs, Divine Providence – but whatever else it takes, it takes perseverance. I did my best to squeeze forty years of Donaldsonville education into half an hour.

Let me tell you, on stage you've got to be bigger than life the way a character is in a play.

"Never quit," I told them. "Never, never, never."

I waved the dollar bill and the nickel.

"I'm not smart, but I'm rich."

They cheered again. They loved it.

My colleagues behind me on the stage stirred uneasily in their chairs. They seemed to feel I had upstaged them, stolen the show.

No doubt each of them had their own version of the story I told, but they lacked the sense of the dramatic I'd acquired from Brother Hugh. They hadn't expected I'd make a hit with these Harvard MBA students.

Lord, forgive me, my heart was dancing.

The dean asked me back to speak for nine more years, till I got to be too old to be a YPO member. Those nine years allowed me to say things I'd wanted to say but hadn't had time for that first go-round, in addition to things I learned along the way.

I told them about perseverance. An MBA from Harvard was a wonderful credential, but you had to have perseverance, too. I told them that all my life I had been learning and teaching that lesson, that for me it was a fundamental belief, proved out by experience over and over. I explained that my education, begun before I ever got to school, way back in the Depression, taught me to never quit.

"The one sure way to fail," I said, "is to quit."

I also talked to these bright young people about the nature of education.

"Education goes on all around us all the time. In my case, a lot of it's been self-education. In fact, most of your education is going to be self-education. And I'll tell you something else that maybe you hadn't thought about. Most of the education that you get right here at this great university is self-education, because what you get from the opportunities provided here is mostly up to you. It's there, but you have to reach out and grab it. Getting an education, whether you get it at a university or the way I have, is hard work."

I wanted to share what I knew.

Building a business from nothing – starting from scratch, with a trickle of cash flow, low reserves, and few intellectual assets – is an uphill fight.

Each MBA class wanted to know how we did it. How do you build a business? How do you build a funeral home and burial insurance business to where it qualifies you for the Young Presidents Organization? You live on potatoes for three months and work eighteen-hour days. Marry Margy. Margy wouldn't let me quit, wouldn't let me fail. For Margy, nothing was ever impossible.

I told the Harvard MBA students how Margy and I built the business slowly and steadily, from when the Commissioner of Insurance wanted to shut us down because our surplus was only one dollar and twenty-five cents. I told them we did it a step at a time, a stop at a time, a sale at a time, an acquisition at a time. With each step we learned.

"How many stops at a nickel a stop do you think it took?"

I wanted them to taste the hot dust and grit of backyards, to walk into dim kitchens with me and to sit at wooden tables and talk insurance. I wanted them to see through my eyes as I looked myself in the mirror and said:

"Ous, just get out there and sell policies. Don't let up. Get up, and knock the sonofabitch out."

I wanted them to do well. To do good. To do well by doing good.

"Think of ways to do better the things you're doing already," I said. "I'm talking about details, about the little things you've got to do right."

I told how we got so we could expand a little bit, and began to purchase other funeral homes. It seemed a good idea to go to once-a-month collections, because this left more time to sell new policies. But with monthly collection of the premium if you didn't get around to collect until after the water, telephone and electric bills came due, there was no money for the insurance. Collect before these bills come due. A small detail that made a big difference.

Then we had to explain to people that some months had four weeks and some five. For five-week months they owed more. "A month's a month," they complained. Well, one in three months has five weeks. So we billed each month for four and one-third weeks. We learned as we went.

Eventually, we got to the top of *Best's Review*'s list of industrial insurance sellers. This had been our aim all along, though if I'd told anyone, they'd have thought I was delusional.

This is education that goes on all around you all the time. These are things you learn slowly, accumulate day by day, a kind of accretion of intellectual capital that you can't get any other way than step by step, stop by stop, nickel by nickel. It's knowledge accumulating just the way compound interest accumulates. The more you know the faster you learn.

"Education," I told them, "isn't just something you get at a school or university. Sometimes you get it reading books on your own. Self-education. I love to read books. There was a time I read a book a night, a voracious reader, starved for knowledge. Education comes from simple patience and perseverance and faith in your endeavor. That's what I'm talking about here."

Of course, I urged them to appreciate the advantages they had. The education they were getting at Harvard, I told them, gave them a great competitive advantage.

"Don't sell this great advantage short," I said.

A brush with the law

I told them the story about how I read so many books that the FBI investigated me, suspecting I might be a communist. This was back in the 1950s, when Senator Joseph McCarthy's Un-American Activities Committee was trying to flush out communists and other potential subversives who might pose a threat to the American way of life, or to national security.

I couldn't afford to buy all those books. So I borrowed the books from the local library, whose resources were very limited. If the library did not have the book I requested, they could send my request on up the line till it reached the Library of Congress in Washington, which, as I understood it, had all the books published in the U.S.

One day I was summoned to appear before investigators in New Orleans.

What could they want with me? What should I say to them? As I sat in the room waiting for the hearing to begin, I noticed there were other people there, and I thought I'd just wait and see what questions the

FBI man asked and how the others answered. But he called my name first.

"Yes, sir," I answered.

I sat at the table in front of the room. The chief investigator leaned toward me over the table. He looked mean and gruff. Last night's jambalaya must have still been on his stomach.

"Mr. Ourso, do you know what happens when you request a book from your library over in Donaldsonville?"

I told him I supposed that if my local library didn't have the book I requested, they ordered it for me from the regional public library in New Orleans, and if the regional library didn't have it, it was ordered from the Library of Congress.

"Mr. Ourso," the investigator said, "our records show you've borrowed more books from the Library of Congress this year than anybody in the country."

"Yes, sir."

"Well, Mr. Ourso, what we'd like to know is what you're doing with all those books."

"I'm reading them," I said. "I'm a voracious reader."

"Are you a communist?" the investigator asked.

"Oh, no sir. I served my country in the war. I'm an American boy from Donaldsonville. I'm not a communist; I'm a reader."

And so they let me go on reading.

I told this story at Harvard to help the students appreciate the advantages this university afforded them.

"When you get your MBAs don't expect success to right away walk up and knock on your door and say, 'May I come in?' No, and another thing: Don't let your education end when you leave Harvard and go out to make your way. In fact, how well you make your way will depend on the education that goes on after you get out there. Education for success happens all along, day by day. Success itself is a process, not a state of being," I offered.

That's what I tried to show them. The long days going door to door, in the blazing sun, in cold rain. Later, after that, once we'd expanded a little, the day-in-and-day-out routine of ten- or twelve- or sometimes eighteen-hour days in the office, poring over policy applications, following up on client complaints, making sure we were providing the best service we could, the best service available.

"Listen," I said, "if you visit Louisiana you'll notice our license plates say 'Sportsman's Paradise,' because we've got some of the best fishing and hunting in the country. But, let me tell you, I never fished or hunted or played golf. There wasn't time."

'The University of Donaldsonville'

During those years I spoke at Harvard, I developed a theme: "You get your diploma at Harvard, but you get your education in Donaldsonville."

The idea had been on my mind during that first speech, but I held it back, fearing that if I blurted it out it would have earned me a reception similar to that earned by the fellow who bragged on his Wharton MBA. And I needed time to figure out exactly what I might really mean by such a statement.

The idea took shape after we began to hire some of the Harvard MBA students as summer interns. Just how did you get your education in Donaldsonville? And how did that Donaldsonville education differ essentially from a Harvard education? I began to think about this a lot in the early seventies.

I admit my ideas about education may be "out of the box." Where did I get all these impossible notions? That I could sell broken toys on the front steps? That I could make a fortune cleaning out attics and sheds? Why did impossible dreams visit me?

One answer is that in Donaldsonville we're naive, but naive in a positive way: We don't know what we can't do. We grew up making do; we weren't burdened with a sense of what was impossible, for that would have stopped great ideas before they started. A Donaldsonville education lets impossible dreams grow unchecked.

First, isn't the mind, the human mind, like an infinitely large container? Now that sounds impossible, doesn't it? A self-contradiction. Because how could a container, which has a limited capacity, however great it may be, be infinitely large? By definition, a container is not infinite.

I think of mental capacity as an infinitely large container. It's a container because it contains all we experience; it's infinite because it can always hold more.

Second, doesn't all our experience flow into this container, where it gets mixed up and blended together? But it's not neat, like a drawer of files, or an accountant's balance sheet. It's more like a drawer into which you put odds and ends that you don't know what to do with but don't want to throw away for fear they might be needed someday.

I think of compound interest, perseverance, and Giannini's story as experiences in the world around me, disconnected from one another, but eventually, by chance, floating about inside my head, having in common only that they occupied the same mind, where all sorts of other stuff had accumulated. What all of that had in common was that it came into my head, my mind. Just by chance it was my particular stream of experience, hence the raw material of my contemplations.

Now, as I see it, this is exactly the great thing about the human mind. It can contain things not necessarily connected in one certain way to everything else in there or to anything else in there, which opens the possibility that what's in there can be connected up in an infinite variety of ways – another way in which this container is infinite.

That's where "thinking out of the box" comes in. Our minds make all kinds of connections among the unconnected experiences in them. The one thing that can hinder this is if we've been pumped full of rules about what can or can't be connected with what. The rules put certain things in certain boxes, and that's what a conventional, formal education does.

Suppose there was a rule that you can't sell broken toys? Or that six ragtag boys from Donaldsonville can't win a district basketball championship? Or if the girl you want to marry is already engaged to a dentist, forget her? Or that you can't start out with $10,000 and compete against the Met and the Pru? Education that gives you too many rules keeps you "thinking in the box."

Donaldsonville was the perfect place for "thinking out of the box," because there was no one around to tell a boy all these rules about what he could or couldn't do. All the unconnected experiences that had flowed into my mind were free to connect up with one another whichever way they chose.

So this is the second part of my notion of education: There are kinds of education that hinder more than help.

Third, what causes us to make the connections we do make? Why did I get my particular notions? Why did General Patton get the impossible, laughable idea that he could turn his 3rd Army around and reach Bastogne in forty-eight hours? It's called focus.

Brother Alton, my high school football coach, hit the nail on the head. Could a one hundred thirty-five pound kid play offensive and defensive guard? Impossible? Not if he had focus.

Focus is a mental quality. Focus gets just the right ingredients of what's in the brain connected up with each other in a way that's unique and useful. Focus organizes, lines things up, so that they all work together in a single direction.

Desire produces focus. My idea to clean attics and sheds depended on my intense desire to collect the scrap paper and iron, a desire motivated by the necessity of making do. I had scrap paper and iron on the brain. The more determined, the more concentrated I got on the task I had set for myself, the more likely some of my mind's accumulated but unconnected contents would combine and crystallize into the idea that I needed right at that moment to achieve the task.

I'd been in attics and sheds. What the attics and sheds contained had flowed into my mind, and got mixed in with everything else that had flowed in over time, where it all drifted about until that summer when my every waking and sleeping moment was focused on the search for scrap, because this was the Depression and we had to make do.

Just like General Patton had to get to Bastogne. He was so focused on what he had to do that he had figured out not one but three ways to do it.

The stuff in our minds, on which this work takes place, pours in to us from all sides. For me it took place in Donaldsonville. Whatever comes to eye or ear floods in. We take it all in, often without realizing it, as we listen, see, touch, smell, taste. Those sensations are the tributaries feeding our mental river, where they are all mixed in the large currents of our thinking. Education of this sort surrounds us; we take it in all the time.

Books extend and multiply these tributaries; with books we can listen, see, touch, smell, and taste as others do. Therefore, one way or the other, I can say that all my life I have been in the process of education, of accumulating and storing, of concentrating and organizing and communicating. One way or the other, learning and teaching, a perpetual student and teacher.

So my education began long before my days at LSU, before my high school years with Brothers Hugh and Alton, and it went on long after I left the university and went to war, and after I came back to Donaldsonville and Margy and I were married and started building the business.

I have always been an aggressive learner. I sought to learn wherever and from whomever I could, and I discovered very early that learning opportunities are everywhere, not all concentrated in one place like a high school classroom, or a university. Many times I found them right on my own doorstep.

It is true that I've been around a bit, and studied at LSU, and I was in the war, and that's all fine and valuable experience. But I learned the most important lessons in Donaldsonville, because those first lessons in Donaldsonville were lessons in the use of my God-given senses.

I learned to take in everything that could be taken in wherever I was. Didn't let anything go to waste. Tucked it away in my mental drawer for later use. From Donaldsonville, my mental springboard, my senses dove into everything.

What did I learn in Donaldsonville? Right on my own doorstep? I learned close and careful observation of what's in front of me, the good of what I could reach out and touch with my own hand. I call this the near-at-hand. In Latin class Brother Hugh might have called it *terra cognita*.

What did I learn when I offered that ball with a hole in it to the little boy? I learned that if he could hold it, if he could touch it, he would want it, with or without the hole.

And his mother, what did she want? I could see she didn't have much money, couldn't afford new toys for the boy. I listened to her carefully, to what she said and to what she didn't say. She worried a new toy would soon be broken, or lost. I could see it in her face. Peace of mind was what she wanted. She wanted relief from worry, from the common anxieties of life. She wanted to be in a world where things couldn't break, where you didn't have to worry about loss.

The ball with the hole in it offered her a different look at things. We don't have a world in which things don't break. Everything in this world eventually breaks. Or gets lost. But here's a way that will worry you less. And isn't that what we all want?

To my way of thinking, burial insurance gives us pretty much the same kind of thing. Our human bodies aren't immortal; eventually we're going to break or be lost, but here's a way of looking at it that will worry us less.

So, though I couldn't have put it into these words then, I offered her peace of mind, less anxiety, in a world awash with cares.

"You won't have to worry about him breaking it, ma'am," I remember telling her.

The lesson? A simple but important lesson. Watch what's going on right at your own doorstep. Watch people. What do they want? Try to give it to them. There are opportunities for learning something useful every day. Look out. Look around. What Russell Conwell said about acres of diamonds goes for education as well. There was a world of education right in Donaldsonville, without which travel would have had little value.

So I told the MBAs at Harvard you get your diploma from Harvard, but you get your education in Donaldsonville. I meant that Donaldsonville represented a special kind of place, not that Donaldsonville was totally unique, but rather that it had certain characteristics that allowed a boy to learn the importance of close and exact observation without being boxed in by rules about what is or is not possible.

I meant that this Donaldsonville education was different in some essential way from a Harvard or Stanford or LSU education, because in Donaldsonville you didn't learn what you couldn't do but rather what you could do. You learned to dream impossible dreams.

I had never had any college courses in economics or in business. I hadn't been introduced to all the quantitative methods of finance and capital budgeting, as business students are. I hadn't been educated in what is impossible, by the numbers or by the book. I figured you can build a company a nickel a stop, twenty stops to the dollar.

Donaldsonville schooled me in dreaming the impossible. I found it was possible to sell broken toys, to collect scrap paper and scrap iron when there seemed to be none to collect, possible to sell seven hundred chickens in a summer, possible for six ordinary boys with funny nicknames to win the district basketball championship, possible to win the girl of my dreams even if she was engaged to be married to a fancy dentist from New Orleans, possible to buy the house of Margy's dreams even if we could only half-afford it, and, yes, possible to build a successful business in competition with the top insurance companies, to be the best of *Best* with more than one billion dollars of insurance in force.

"The Impossible Dream" is a theme song for me, expressing what I have learned and what I try to teach.

Security's internship program

Each time I spoke at Harvard, I invited the MBA students to come to Donaldsonville for a summer as MBA interns at Security Industrial Insurance.

"Get a Donaldsonville education," I said.

Many accepted my invitation.

In fact, they went on accepting it long after I graduated from the Young Presidents Organization. Every summer for twenty-five years, we hired MBA students as interns. They came from all over, including UCLA, Stanford, LSU and Wharton, but mostly from Harvard, recommended to us by the dean. Usually they'd grown up in big cities like Boston, New York, Philadelphia, Los Angeles, or maybe Atlanta or Houston. They wanted to know how business could possibly be done out in the country by country people. Growing up in the city, surrounded by city people, they had naturally come to think that business success was achieved by city people in the city. Even if they'd grown up in rural areas, they hadn't associated business success with the country. Big business was a city thing, in their minds.

"Let me tell you," I'd say to our interns, "the ways to be successful are as infinite as the capacity of the human mind. Success does not depend on where you are but on who you are and what you do with who you are."

I got this from reading Russell Conwell. He was talking to a bunch of people in Philadelphia, some of whom had said they couldn't succeed because they weren't in New York. If you can't succeed in Philadelphia, he told them, you won't succeed in New York.

That goes for education as well. If you can't get an education in Donaldsonville, you won't get an education at Harvard either.

The value of intellectual assets

The idea of the impossible being possible was the core of our MBA internship. I wanted to give these young business-bent people what I had learned.

I shared, for example, lessons I learned about intellectual assets. I couldn't over-stress the importance of intellectual assets. The interns, no matter where they came from, hadn't given much thought to intellectual assets because these assets didn't appear on the balance sheets in their accounting and finance classes. From the outset, my Donaldsonville experience showed me that intellectual assets usually amounted to more than half the value of an acquisition. Think about that: More than half the acquisition's value never appeared on paper, nor was it referred to explicitly in any of the negotiations leading to the acquisition.

What did I mean by intellectual assets, the interns wanted to know. How could such abstract assets have tangible value? The subject of acquisitions and mergers intensely interested the interns. How did these intellectual assets figure in my strategy of acquisitions and mergers? If they weren't on the balance sheet, how did you account for them? Were they depreciable? To help them understand, I offered a simple analogy:

"When you arrived here, what did you bring with you, besides your toothbrush and a fresh change of clothes? Pretty much all you brought with you, besides a few personal belongings, were your intellectual assets, the education you've absorbed up to now. Not just your education in schools, your whole education. What you know, what you can do, and what you can learn to do by building on what you already know and already can do. And also the character you've acquired, your habits and attitude, and everything that goes into what we call a work ethic. In short, I'm pretty much talking about who you are. Now tell me if you don't think all that adds up to something solid, deserving consideration."

The intellectual assets of a funeral home or insurance company, I explained further, are the competencies the managers and employees of that company have built up over the years the company has been doing business. They include all the employees' and the managers' experience and training, the instincts they have developed, even things they know without knowing how they've come to know them, what someone has called tacit knowledge.

Intellectual assets include knowledge of the town the company is in and of the people who live there. What are the customs and the needs of the townspeople? People born and reared in a town absorb this knowledge from birth and take it in year after year. So think about the accumulation of intellectual assets in a company where all the employees and managers are homegrown and have been there since high school. Talk about acres of diamonds!

Before negotiations begin, do your homework. The interns knew about the research that usually went into an acquisition or merger: the costs, the revenues and the surpluses; mortality rates; and all the other things that were going to affect the flow of cash and the build-up of reserves. But what about how long the company has been in business, how long the managers and employees have been working there, and how long they've lived in that town? Are they married? Do they have children? What did their fathers and mothers do? Interview the sales people, on the telephone and in person. Look at letters they've written and received.

Do this to assess the worth of the company's intellectual assets, which, though they're not recorded on the balance sheet, nevertheless have a tremendous impact on the income statement. It takes close and careful observation of people, listening to what they say, listening to what they don't say. The ability to assess intellectual assets is itself an intellectual asset accrued over the years. I could tell the interns about it and give them a summer's practice in it, but, like compound interest, it accrues slowly and steadily over the years. For each of us, the value of our intellectual assets accrues a nickel a stop, twenty stops to the dollar.

Don't talk intellectual assets during merger negotiations. Negotiate the physical and monetary assets in the balance sheet's left column. The price you arrive at refers to those.

But don't discount these assets either. Even though they're not explicitly mentioned, they have an impact. They can make an otherwise unattractive merger or acquisition very appealing.

The presence of these intellectual assets means that the acquired company can immediately begin to show progress and growth, since you don't have to put everything on hold while you train their people, which costs money. If the only assets we acquired were those listed on the balance sheet, many of the mergers we completed would probably have been beyond reach.

The presence of the intellectual assets means you can reasonably offer to pay more for a company than it looks to be worth on paper. How much I'm going to be willing to pay for a company depends on its total worth, which includes the worth of its intellectual assets. It's not rocket science; it's common sense.

The more the company is worth, the more I am willing to pay. The more I am willing to pay, the more I can bid. The more I can bid, the better the chances that my bid will be the one the company accepts. What looks to be an impossible acquisition on paper turns out to be possible after all.

We built Security Industrial Insurance Company on this fundamental truth. When we acquired another funeral home or burial insurance business, we acquired physical assets such as buildings and monetary assets such as reserves, but the most valuable assets we acquired were the intellectual assets. This is because the intellectual assets, properly nurtured and cultivated, were what was going to make that business more and more profitable.

If I included these assets in my analysis and my competitors didn't, or if I estimated the value of these assets more accurately than did my competitors, I had a competitive advantage. My own Donaldsonville education – which went on all the time all around me and had made me an observer and close listener – gave me this competitive advantage.

"That's the bottom line," I told them.

The interns liked that.

One of the interns I remember most vividly was Mike Schott, a strikingly handsome young fellow from Michigan who'd been an All American football player at Ohio State before going on to Harvard for his MBA. I took Mike with me to New York to secure a loan from Chase Manhattan Bank for $28 million, which we proposed to use in the purchase of First National Life Insurance.

Mike was a tremendous help. We had all our charts and graphs showing Security Industrial's record of profit growth and return on investment. (We were talking to bankers, remember.) And we got the loan.

But our evening of self-congratulations before heading back to Donaldsonville was premature. We succeeded in convincing Chase Manhattan of the soundness of our venture, but our bid for First National Life, although it seemed to be the best bid, was not accepted because of insider opposition. We were outsiders from Donaldsonville.

Lesson: Sometimes you can do everything right and still not win.

In our negotiations to buy funeral homes and/or insurance companies, talking across the table to representatives of these companies we didn't speak of acquisitions. Instead we spoke of mergers. This conveyed that we regarded the business as an ongoing concern, not something about to be shut down, or taken over and changed and transformed. In the negotiations, we always tried to say things that made the present owners feel good about themselves. We made a point of praising what was praiseworthy. We kept as much of the business in place as we could, especially the people with background and know-how.

A big part of the interns' Donaldsonville education took place as we prepared for these negotiations. The interns, as I've said, were adept at all the aspects of financial analysis. They understood about market share, cash flows, net present value, and cost of capital. They helped us greatly in researching and calculating these things. And Lord knows, if you haven't done this homework, you better back up and do it, because without this knowledge you will make some big mistakes, in addition to seriously weakening your credibility and ability to negotiate.

Nevertheless, there were other things, not covered in traditional MBA programs, at which the interns were less adept. For example, a large part of a negotiation's success depends on the language you use to talk to the representatives of the other company. Suppose the people representing the other company are accountants. You need to know this before you arrive at the negotiating table. It's information important to your negotiation's success, just as a knowledge of a young wife's worry about making do if anything happened to her husband was key to my success as a seller of burial insurance. I had to find words to speak to her concerns. I had to know when to sit silent and let an unspoken thought sink in.

So know the accountant's language. What does the accountant spend time doing? What are his or her main worries? To find the right words, you have to see the segment of the world the accountant sees every day through the accountant's eyes. There are times when the best thing to do is sit silent while the accountant turns over an idea or proposal in his mind.

The same goes for lawyers, if that's who's across the table from you, or for bankers, or for the owners themselves. Accountants think about how assets are valued and about accounts receivable, accounts payable, operating budgets, and such. Lawyers worry about taxes. Bankers think about liens and other possible encumbrances.

The owners are the most complex of all, but know about them. Are they members of the same family? Parents and children? Brothers? Cousins? What you put on the table, how you lay it out, will all depend on who the owners are. Typically, owners have a strong interest in growth; they want to see the bidding company's track record. If you're not talking their language, haven't imagined their point of view, your chances of success go down. Don't judge present management. Hear what you're saying from their seat at the table.

Role-playing: A negotiating tool

Once we collected all the financial information and knew who we would be talking with, we all got together in a back room at the office and played out the various parts. We engaged in role-playing – the interns, my staff people and me. The interns had studied cases, especially the Harvard students, but they hadn't done this kind of acting. It wasn't acting Hamlet, as we did for Brother Hugh, but the idea was very similar. You had to imagine yourself into the other person's point of view, see through that person's eyes, smell a rat if the person smelled a rat, except that now, unlike Brother Hugh's exercises, we didn't have a script. We had to create the script as we went, based on what we knew about the person's character and the situation.

What would this particular banker, in his particular situation, want to ask us and what kind of answer would convince him? We spent hours playing out the various roles, until we had asked and answered every conceivable question we might be asked in the actual negotiating session. By the end of the summer our interns were very good at this kind of role-playing. I think they enjoyed it.

Our acquisition of Southern National Life Insurance Company of Baton Rouge in 1971 provides a good example of role-playing's importance. That summer we had as an intern a tall boy named Steve Hyde, who has since become a very successful financial consultant to nursing homes. Steve was a Harvard MBA student. He grew up in north Louisiana. The son of a poor widow, he didn't have much money. On a hot day in June, wearing the only suit he owned, a heavy brown corduroy, in which he was sweating noticeably, he arrived in Donaldsonville on his motorcycle. Steve played a major role in the acquisition of Southern National.

The major owners were two elderly sisters, both widows, each of whom owned 24% of the company's stock, which a bank held in trust for them. The sister with whom we were going to negotiate was a slight, small woman not more than five feet tall. We'd heard from reliable sources she was a shrewd businesswoman and expected that whatever bid we made, she would ask for more. If we said $25 a share, she would say $30. Actually, we were prepared to pay $27.50. But if we began by offering $27.50, you could bet we'd end up with around $30.

We also knew that our offer of $27.50 would be approved by the bank, which much preferred to hold the cash rather than the shares in trust, since the cash could earn money while they held it. The company's attorney, too, favored the sale. Before we sat down at the table, we knew we had the support of all the major players - except one.

All week long, in preparation for our day of reckoning with this tough woman, Steve and I practiced our parts. We would be sitting across the table from her. I would make an offer of $25. She would angrily retort, "Thirty!" Together, Steve and I would leap from our chairs, rise to our full height, tower over her, and exclaim, "Thirty dollars!" in shock and disbelief. We went over and over it until our bodies rose as one and our voices exclaimed as one, "Thirty dollars!"

Well, at the negotiations the woman, hard as nails in so many previous transactions, sank back into her leather chair when we spoke up in unison. Then she readily accepted our counteroffer of $27.50.

Of course, we sometimes fell short of the acquisition we were pursuing. But we succeeded frequently enough to demonstrate the effectiveness of role-playing. I tried to teach the interns to dream big; to think big thoughts; to believe they can win. And then to go out and do what it takes. I didn't let them forget that the dreams come true only after much hard work has been done.

You've got to have your ducks in a row, your cost graphs and premium charts ready to line up to illustrate the advantages of the merger. And you've got to know in advance who it is you'll be talking with, so you're ready to talk balance sheets and cash flow or contracts and contingencies or records and assets, depending on who you're dealing with.

With all that swimming around in your mind, all the unconnected things and ideas that have flooded in, your imagination, unfettered by all the rules about what can and can't be done, has its materials and is ready to go to work on the big impossible dream. Here, your Donaldsonville education comes in handy.

The interns were a world of help to us in gathering all the information we needed and organizing it into a nice, neat package of graphs, charts and tables of numbers. We learned from them as they learned from us.

But what Donaldsonville added to their education was the principle that once you got all the information together, and you knew the company in your sights was worth pursuing, and what it should take to get it, then, even if it looked like winning the bid was a long shot, you'd talk positively to yourself:

"Never mind what all the numbers say about my chances, I know what it will take and I can put together the winning bid."

And off we'd go, me with my old, worn briefcase, "Old Lucky," and the interns with the charts and graphs tucked under their arms.

At the summer's beginning I gave each of the interns an "entrepreneur's starter kit." It was a little canvas tote bag full of slogans on bumper stickers – like "IF IT IS TO BE, IT'S UP TO ME" and "NEVER QUIT, NEVER, NEVER, NEVER" – and a mirror so they could take a good look each morning at "ME." Among the items was a list of books that included Napoleon Hill's *Think and Grow Rich*, Russell Conwell's *Acres of Diamonds*, Dale Carnegie's *How To Win Friends and Influence People*, and a biography of A.P. Giannini, the founder and architect of Bank of America.

All of these books had deeply influenced me. I read them many times, each time finding something I hadn't gotten in previous readings. I didn't just read, I submerged myself, trying to soak up all that was there, to absorb and digest, until the book's substance became united with my own substance.

I identified closely with Giannini, for he dreamed impossible dreams and accomplished them. I thought of him as my role model. A sort of older brother, my mentor.

Giannini and I differed greatly in outward aspects: He was the son of an Italian immigrant, just off the boat in San Francisco, a street vender of fruits and vegetables; I was the descendant of the old Spanish Del Ourse, living in Donaldsonville, and in the funeral home business. But we were fundamentally alike: brothers in that we were both outsiders who took unconventional paths to success.

He inspired me. I figured that if this Italian street vendor-turned-banker by dint of perseverance and imagination, coupled with the powers of compound interest and strategic acquisition, could build a Bank of America, then I could do the same with an insurance business in Donaldsonville.

You couldn't start out any more humbly than did Giannini. In a community of Italian vendors, denied because of their status as immigrants the privilege of conventional banking in the city's banks, Giannini became their banker, pushing his wooden vending cart from merchant to merchant, lending cash in their time of need, their sole resource. In this he prospered and founded his own bank, the Bank of Italy, where he continued to serve his constituency.

The San Francisco earthquake of 1906, in which he rescued his reserve funds from his vault, left him one of the few bankers standing in the shattered town capable of supplying the funds needed for rebuilding. He might be an outsider still, but they needed his money. And so he began to acquire other banks, to enlarge his holdings, reaching beyond San Francisco. He dreamed impossible dreams.

If he could dream impossible dreams in San Francisco, why couldn't I in Donaldsonville? Why couldn't I acquire insurance companies as Giannini acquired banks? I had the education for it, didn't I?

CHAPTER 5

It Takes Big People
To Build A Big Company

A FTER ACQUIRING AN INSURANCE COMPANY OR funeral home our administrative people looked after its financial assets, its bonds and reserves and cash. I focused on its people, its intellectual assets. I considered the people to be the most valuable part.

The acquisition's success depended on the caliber, expertise and motivation of its people. If the people were well trained and had experience in their jobs, we had a head start because we wouldn't need to wait till they learned the ropes to begin improving productivity. My job was to show them they could be successful and to motivate them. So the first thing I did was go over and personally welcome the new company's people to Security Industrial Insurance.

I'd take out our charts and tables and show them the record of our growth, internal as well as by mergers and acquisitions. I'd tell them they had joined a winning team. This made them feel good about themselves; it boosted their self-esteem and confidence. Just being on a winning team powerfully motivates people to do their best.

As I told the interns, more than half the value of the acquisition is in its intellectual assets, that is, in the competencies and motivation of its employees and managers, particularly its salespeople. Moreover, a healthy level of self-esteem adds force to people's competencies. I've also found that if you let people know you expect them to be successful, they are more likely to be successful. If they believe they'll be successful, that's

93

how it usually turns out. It's a self-fulfilling prophecy.

I made enhancement of our people's self-esteem my specialty. Ask Chef John Folse about my "pre-meal classes." We called them sales meetings, but they were more like tent revival meetings. We'd book the big dining room of LaFitte's Landing Restaurant in Donaldsonville and invite all the sales people. Nobody was going to miss a meal at LaFitte's. First the meeting, then the meal.

Let me tell you, I was fired up. I couldn't stand still, pouncing like a tiger back and forth across the room, pounding my fist into my hand. My dramatic imagination took hold of me. I told our people:

"You're the best, you're the best."

And I meant it. That got them up on the chairs, shouting, cheering. I told them they were the company.

"Represent it as if you own it. When you're standing in front of a customer, you are the company. Me, I just pay the bills, and make sure you have what you need. I give you what you need to sell. But, remember, when you're in front of that woman or man, the customer, you are the company."

I worked up such a sweat I had to loosen my tie and pull it off to the side so I could breathe deeper.

"It is your company. You make it what it is."

As for John Folse, he picked up on this immediately and took a whole new tack on the motivation of his serving staff. He had four or five waiters, each of whom had a section of tables in the dining room. After seeing my revival meeting, John did his own version. He spoke excitedly to his waiters:

"Think of your four tables as your own little restaurant. I supply the plates and silverware and napkins and tables and food, whatever you need, but it's your little restaurant, and how well it does depends on you."

Without adding staff, they doubled their sales. Motivating people and building their self-esteem made all the difference.

In July 1993, our newsletter, *Security Progress*, announced that "on June 25, 1993 the company reached $1,000,369,353" insurance in force.

"It may seem to be a coincidence that this mark was achieved in the month before our 45th anniversary ... but it took a lot of hard work by a lot of people for a lot of years," the article stated.

It was a dream come true, which could not have come true without our people – without our people believing in themselves and in Security Industrial.

At its peak, Security Industrial employed 1,500 people, including agents, staff managers, district and regional managers, and all of the office people in all of our companies throughout Louisiana. Let me tell you, every one of them was important to the achievement of that billion dollar dream.

In our first year, 1948, we had less than $250,000 insurance in force; in 1993, after 45 years, we had more than one billion. We had soared like a rocket to the top of the A.M. *Best Review's* list of best-performing industrial insurance companies. We ranked first in amount of insurance in force, exceeding the expectations of everyone but ourselves. We were a company of overperformers.

Some of the big people who built Security Industrial

To build a big company you need big people. Big people have high self-esteem and confidence in their ability to do their jobs well. Big people are motivated by the desire to excel. They love to win. Big people are ordinary people who accomplish extraordinary things. They overperform. I'm a believer in overperformers.

Argie Kemp, for several years our leading agent, was an ordinary person who did extraordinary things. Argie lived quietly in the country outside Amite, where she raised a few chickens and pigs. Her husband was disabled; necessity made her the family's main breadwinner.

Our district manager, L.R. Scott, had recruited Argie and started her out on a small debit route. (Sometimes referred to as a collection route, with a debit route the sales agent goes door to door periodically, in a specified territory, to collect insurance premiums from his/her policyholders.)

Argie knew just about everyone in the vicinity of Amite, and she immediately set about getting people on her route to convert their term life policies to whole life. The whole life policy meant higher premiums, but it brought the policyholder greater advantages. That was Argie's specialty: converting term policies to whole life policies. Selling insurance was what Argie was cut out to do.

People trusted this quiet, hardworking woman, apparently so much like themselves. Before coming to work for us, she displayed no extraordinary talent. She was a seemingly ordinary country woman in her forties. But given the opportunity, she revealed a talent for sales neither she nor anyone else suspected she had. She made a very comfortable living for her family.

Another overperformer was Irene Giroir. She lived in Houma and became one of our best sales managers, excellent at training and retaining agents.

Irene herself was hired as a builder, an agent who builds the route starting from scratch with cold calls. Soon Irene had established a route and built it up till it required more than one agent. She was so successful a builder that we promoted her to sales manager. She got to be sales manager to twelve agents, most of whom did very well.

Irene was a leader and, like Argie, a person with significant talents she hadn't known she had. And Irene's overperformance was all the more extraordinary because she managed it without the benefit of a formal education. What small degree of literacy she had acquired came from adult education classes and from helping her children with their homework. Nevertheless, she was a splendid problem-solver.

"Here's what I would do," she would say. Most of her ideas succeeded. Faced with a problem, she cut right to the critical issue. She asked good questions.

However, Irene did not want to be district manager, fearing that her deficiency in literacy would embarrass her in that position. She remained a sales manager, although I am confident she would have performed well as a district manager. While she was a sales manager, the Office of the Insurance Commissioner decided any agent who wanted to sell industrial fire insurance would be required to pass a test. Irene had to receive special permission to take the test orally, but passed with high marks. This ordinary woman accomplished extraordinary things, despite significant handicaps.

Irene's district manager was a woman named Mary Horton, also from Houma. She too had been hired as a builder and had quickly built her route to the point that it needed more agents. She was so good at recruiting and training agents that we promoted her to district manager.

Mary's special talent was selecting people as agents. She had her own unique method, which consisted of hiring women who had worked as bartenders. Why might bartenders be expected to be especially successful as salespeople? It's really not difficult to see. As a bartender your possibilities are extremely limited. Wages are minimal and not likely to rise quickly, if at all, no matter how hard you work. For the person inclined to work hard, it's a frustrating job.

But hard work pays off in the insurance business, because you get a percentage of the premiums you collect. As agents, these women could increase what they earned by simply working harder. Their capacity for hard work was the only limit on what they could earn. Earnings grew as the customer base expanded. So the deal Mary offered had great appeal for women in that situation, if they were hard workers. Mary always hired women from that background. And her hiring practices put us on the frontier when it came to hiring and promoting women.

H.P. Williams was our top agent of all time, an overperformer's overperformer. H.P. was a partner in and funeral director of the Williams and Southall Funeral Home in Bertrandville, which is ten or twelve miles south of Donaldsonville. Though a man of little formal education, H.P. was an enormously talented salesman. During his fifteen years with us, his intuition for people's needs and desires and his hard work made him our most productive agent.

To all appearances, H.P. was an ordinary man. But he had broad and deep human talents. H.P was a conservative black man, very modest and quiet, as is fitting for a funeral director. He always dressed well. Hot as it gets in south Louisiana, I never saw him when he didn't have on a suit and tie. He managed to stay cool. He didn't hurry. When he talked with you, you had his full attention. Everywhere he went, he carried his rate book with him in his suit jacket's inside pocket, always ready for the opportunity to sell a policy.

According to H.P.'s gospel, readiness was as important as opportunity itself. Week in and week out, H.P.'s name was in the top spot on the agent column of *Security Progress*. By some stroke of luck or circumstance, another agent might top H.P.'s weekly production, but H.P. would be back in the number one slot the following week. His quietness was deceptive. He was a hell of a competitor.

H.P. loved to excel. He sold so much insurance that he made more money than I did, though I owned the company. His annual income from commissions probably exceeded seventy thousand dollars in days when most men would have considered themselves comfortable with twenty-five thousand. H.P.'s debit route became the largest on record. It got so large that he could hardly make all the collections by himself. I don't know how, but somehow he managed it.

Still, for H.P. it wasn't simply commission money that drove him; it was the desire for esteem, both self-esteem and the esteem of his fellow agents and of his community. As H.P. saw it, success earned him esteem. Money – what his money bought – was just his way of posting the score.

H.P. was born and reared in the little black community of Bertrandville outside of Paincourtville down on Bayou Lafourche. Country people like H.P. have a strong work ethic. Because they have to work so hard for what they get, country people appreciate what they have and what people do for them. I've found country people to be the most loyal people in the world. Treat them right and they'll stay with you through thick and thin.

In communities like Bertrandville or Paincourtville or Donaldsonville, everybody knows and helps everybody else. Regardless of religion, race, national origin, or any other accident of birth. If somebody loses a mule, neighbors will come over and help out with spring plowing. If your shed or barn or, Lord help you, your house burns down, most of the community will be there the next day to help you build a new one – even if it means taking time away from their own work. And everybody appreciates the help.

Country people have been caring for one another for generations. This is how they insured themselves against life's catastrophes before the advent of insurance. God bless them, there's nothing that comes near the loyalty country people show you if you help them and treat them well.

Country people have a natural love of growing things. If you've got a growing company, they'll stay with you. They're not fickle; they're not always looking to move on to something that might look better or easier. They'd rather live and work close to where they grew up. They want to be close to their families and friends, who nurtured and taught them, the people who took care of them when they were sick, the people they cared for in turn when the need arose. Now, a small community can't offer a lot of opportunity for work, other than farm work, which is getting scarcer, so what opportunity there is is valued and appreciated.

My advice is to hire country men or women, encourage them, treat them with respect, build their self-esteem. They'll appreciate what you do for them and repay you with loyalty and hard work. They've grown up accustomed to hard work. These are my kind of people.

H.P. Williams was a smart worker, though he probably didn't have any formal education past the eighth grade in a one-room country schoolhouse in Bertrandville. He never ceased to ask me questions.

"Mr. Ourso, what would you say if a lady says, 'Now's just not a good time to start paying on a policy'?" Or, "I talked to a lady and she said she had some money put aside for funeral expenses for herself or her husband, whoever happened to be the first to go. What would you tell her?" He asked me questions every time I saw him. He eventually acquired a ready answer to every objection a prospective client could possibly raise. He always thanked me for my answer, and I believe he usually took my advice.

H.P. sold insurance seven days a week. Sundays he went to three churches. Lord knows he was a truly humble and religious man, but his zealous church attendance advanced his interests in more than the heavenly sphere. Going to church was great promotion for his funeral home. When it comes to bereavement, people want to go to a member of their own congregation, someone they know well and trust.

H.P.'s quiet manner made people trust him. When he spoke, always in a low, soft voice, people leaned closer and listened. He had a gift. He touched people and spoke to their needs and desires. And when the time came, when some loved one passed on, they called H.P. and he came to the bereaved family's house himself and called the coroner and helped with the many arrangements that had to be made. H.P.'s work went beyond being a business to deep caring for the people he served.

H.P. always went the extra mile. Even though he was an owner and the funeral director and had employees assigned the various required duties, he made it to nearly every funeral that took place in the Williams and Southall Funeral Home. He personally consoled the family in mourning.

The people who attended the funeral could see the kind attention the family received from the director himself, and when their time of bereavement came, they came to H.P and Williams and Southall.

So I say that with big people like H.P., Argie, Irene, and Mary you can build a big company. With people like these, you can accomplish great things, things that others only dream of accomplishing.

Don't pay attention to people who say it can't be done. Just go find some good country people – who have grown up in communities where hard work is a way of life – and show them that they are people deserving of respect, individuals who can succeed and grow.

Do everything you can to build up their self-esteem. Let them know right off that they've joined a winning team and that you expect them to succeed. So, as I said earlier, every time we acquired a new company, that's the first thing I did.

"Welcome to Security Industrial. Let me tell you one thing: You've just joined a winning team. Our dream is one billion dollars of life insurance in force," I'd tell them.

Then I handed out copies of *Think and Grow Rich* or *Acres of Diamonds*.

What a difference accomplishment makes in people's lives. Day-by-day successful effort, even if each day's effort by itself is not spectacular, can accumulate and accumulate until it makes a huge difference in how people come to think about themselves. One of my own great rewards has been knowing that some of what we did at Security Industrial made a big difference in the lives of people who worked with us. The success of your people is another way of keeping score.

Belle Andrews, a librarian in Kentwood, had been selling insurance for us part-time. Belle, a country woman, a widow, had a son she wanted to send to college. On a librarian's salary and the pocket money her insurance commissions brought her, college for her son appeared impossible.

"Belle, why don't you sell insurance full-time? You could make enough money to send your boy to college," I suggested.

"You think so, Mr. Ourso?"

"Selling insurance, the harder you work, the more you earn," I added.

She hadn't considered this before. Her salary as a librarian was steady, but it was pretty much fixed. It wasn't going to get much bigger. Being a full-time agent offered her a better life for her son and herself. It made her dream of sending her son to college possible.

She quit her job as librarian and came to work for us full-time. Not only did she send her boy to college but also to medical school, including a specialty in ophthalmology. He's got a practice now in Houston. But my pleasure in telling this story is not so much in the son's success as in his mother's and the way it built her self-esteem and confidence. Once she saw what she could do, she became one of our very good sales people, not an H.P. Williams, but consistently up near the top of our weekly agent list in *Security Progress*. She was with me from the time her son graduated from high school until after he established his ophthalmology practice in Houston, after which she retired.

She kept me up to date on her son's academic and professional progress, and I could tell she felt good about what she had accomplished. The son's achievement became the scoreboard of the mother's success.

When we passed the one billion dollar mark, I thought about Belle, and I can tell you I'm grateful to her for her loyalty and hard work for Security Industrial.

I've got lots of these stories. I inherited some of my mother's love of storytelling. I can tell a similar story about Odell Darnell, a black woman whose daughter, Jonell, is now an OB-GYN doctor practicing in New Orleans. Jonell can tell you how much her mother enjoyed our sales seminars in Las Vegas or Mexico City or Miami, because Odell always brought her along. Black people in Donaldsonville in Odell's time rarely had a chance to achieve in one generation what she and her daughter achieved. Jonell remembers her mother's pride in that achievement. For years Odell was in our top 10%. How she loved that trip to Las Vegas!

For all these people, the accomplishment of what seemed impossible dreams lifted their self-esteem, which enabled them to dream even more impossible dreams. It was a spiral of success.

From the start, I've been fortunate to have the people I've had with me. Alvin Richard, our first bookkeeper, stayed with us forty-eight years. His father, who delivered bread in the French-speaking village of Pierre Part, was the first agent we hired. Alvin had been in the class ahead of mine at Catholic High. After the war he worked as a bookkeeper in Napoleonville. I asked him if he wanted to come to work for us.

The day he arrived, he asked me:

"Where are the books?"

We didn't have any books; I had yet to drum up some business. So, although we'd hired Alvin as a bookkeeper, I took him canvassing with me, which was just about every day. We got terribly hot and thirsty. Alvin would bring little spam hot dogs and bread and water, and that was our lunch. Canvassing in those early days was discouraging, but Alvin stuck it out and eventually did get to keep books. For many years he was my right-hand man. In the early years, when we acquired small companies, Alvin's expertise was invaluable. His talent was managing small companies.

When we began to acquire larger companies, John Fritz took over as right-hand man and financial manager. The job had simply gotten bigger. Fritz, a University of Texas at Austin graduate, had been a financial officer with Southern National Life Insurance Co. for 20 years by the time we acquired that company in 1971. Before that he had been an auditor for the Louisiana Department of Insurance. He brought with him intellectual assets far more valuable than those we paid for when we acquired Southern National Life Insurance. John became our chief accounting and auditing administrator.

He suited us from the top of his head right down to the well-maintained soles of his shoes. Like H.P., John was a meticulous dresser. He always wore a coat and tie – in case he might have to go talk with someone about an acquisition. You wouldn't catch John Fritz with holes in his shoes. In outward appearance he was an ordinary man, but his intellect was extraordinarily sharp. He was conservative, experienced, of high integrity, and excellent at analyzing the financial statements of prospective acquisitions. John had a sure instinct for economies and savings. In these he was my most trusted advisor.

Our debates about acquisitions were much enriched by John's insights, which he delivered in his slow Texas drawl, after careful attention to what others had to say. Nobody would call him wishy-washy. Though he did more listening than talking, he always got around to speaking his mind. He was not inflexible, but once he came to a position, after very careful consideration of several lines of thought, he stuck to it, argued it strongly. John Fritz was one of Security's most valued intellectual assets.

D an Esquivel was one of our most successful district managers. H.P. worked quietly and unobtrusively. Dan was the opposite. "Outgoing" and "forward" describes his style.

He didn't start out in sales, though. He came to us as an accountant, and he worked in the front office. But if one of our debit routes fell vacant I'd send him out on it until we could hire an agent. I remember Dan's first outing of this sort. He couldn't have been more than twenty-six years old, a newly hired accountant. A route fell open in Ponchatoula, a quiet town northwest of New Orleans. Dan was anxious and nervous. No sales experience, but he was willing to try. Eagerly, he headed out the door. But suddenly he turned around and came back in.

"How do you get to Ponchatoula?" he wanted to know.

A Donaldsonville boy, he hadn't done any traveling to speak of beyond the immediate area around Donaldsonville. I doubt he'd even been to New Orleans more than once or twice.

"Get a map," I told him. The boy needed to learn to be resourceful, to get out on his own. He needed to do some traveling.

He got a map and found his way. Once in Ponchatoula he had another problem: He had no idea how the town itself was laid out, which streets were where. He figured the best way to find his way around was to hire a local person to go on the route with him, which he did for a couple of dollars. The time he saved was worth more than the couple of dollars.

Dan grew up in the company. He was with us for thirty-six years, much of that time as an accountant, though eventually he moved over to sales as a district manager. He had the kind of confident personality that could inspire confidence in others. He became an excellent district sales manager, among our top performers in this category. Dan revealed himself to be a person of multiple talents, so I could rely on him for jobs from cold calling to troubleshooting. His trip to Ponchatoula was typical: He would find a way to get the job done. From Dan you got two hundred percent effort.

Along the way, I had the opportunity to help Dan and his family in a time of need. Dan and his wife, Elma, had a little girl named Dolly, who had been sickly from the time she was three. At fourteen, there still was no clear diagnosis of her illness. Dan and Elma didn't have the money to seek the kind of medical expertise Dolly seemed to require. So one day I called Dan into my office and asked him if he'd mind if I tried to find his daughter the kind of help she needed at Ochsner's Hospital in New Orleans. Dan and Elma gratefully allowed me to do this. At Ochsner's, the girl was accurately diagnosed and properly treated. I insisted on paying for this.

When you've got good people, you have an obligation to take care of them. Dan and Elma never ceased to appreciate this, and frankly I have always been grateful I had the ability and the opportunity to help them.

Dan stayed until we sold the company in 1996. Loyal? Dan was tops. I've never worked with a better person on that score.

When I think about Chick Morris, our first agency director, I think about the virtue of self-confidence. Agency director was our top marketing position. But Chick's belief in himself was clear from the start, when he came to work for us as an agent. Here was a young fellow, with a wife, Camilla, and a little girl. Camilla was expecting a second child. Like Margy, she came from White Castle. Eventually she and Chick had five or six children, all girls. Two days after Chick came to work for us, he drove up in a brand new, shiny, two-door Plymouth sedan. Of course, he hadn't bought that car for cash; he was counting on the commissions he knew he was going to earn on sales he had yet to make. He never doubted he would do it.

But what a salesman! Let a prospect suggest that she'd already taken precautions and set aside what she'd need for funeral expenses - no need to invest in one of those burial insurance policies - and Chick was ready, loaded for bear.

"But suppose your husband makes it for another five, ten, fifteen, even twenty years? Five thousand dollars won't get you much after inflation gets done with you. And you better believe, it's not if, it's when," he would say excitedly.

And he'd sell another policy. Not exactly H.P.'s style, nor quite mine either, though I guess I come closer to Chick than to H.P, but it got the job done. He had the sense of humor to go with this hard-sell approach, and the kind of outgoing personality and good looks that made it all come together and work.

Chick's strong point was follow-up. Give him something to do, and you could count it as done. I had to tell him only once. Nobody was more dependable. He did well enough at sales, well enough to pay off that Plymouth in short order.

I soon saw, however, that his talent wasn't so much for sales as it was for organization and administration. Chick took care of the details; nothing got by him unattended. There are a lot of people who make big plans. There are fewer who follow up. There are still fewer who do the details as Chick did. That's not your typical salesperson.

Salespeople are strong closers. Details are cleaned up later, after the sale is closed. Chick had his strengths as a closer, but he was first and foremost a detail person. I appreciated that because I'm a detail person myself. I like to have all the details nailed down, secure, no loose ends turning up. I don't want things to jump up and bite me like a cotton-mouth in a swamp.

Chick grew up through the company from agent to staff manager to district manager to regional manager and finally to the top sales management position. He was the first one to fill that position, so you could say of Chick that he grew and matured as the company grew and matured. With Chick I didn't have to worry about the snakes in the swamp.

Another outstanding director of sales agents was my own nephew, Sidney Harp, who worked with us for twenty-six years. He sat in every chair, as they say. Sidney, my sister Elsie's boy, graduated from Nicholls State University in Thibodaux, having majored in business management. As a college student, he worked at one of our funeral homes, starting as a bookkeeper. In six months he moved over to claims. Soon Sidney was helping out in the field after hours with a debit route. Though he was a quiet boy, he had personality; he came across as very sincere, and therefore he turned into an excellent salesman.

In December 1974 we acquired a funeral home in Baton Rouge, and I sent Sidney over to run it. I simply gave him a rate book and three agents.

"I want you to build a staff there," I told him.

Sidney could handle assignments like that. He went on up the line, from agent to staff manager to district manager to regional manager and finally became our agency director. As did Dan Esquivel and Chick Morris, Sidney literally grew up in and with the company. He might have been the best recruiter we ever had, and we had some good ones. He stayed with us until we sold the company. Sidney did something none of our other managers has ever equaled: He set a record of fifty consecutive months of growth in sales.

Another of the more memorable employees of our company was Dot Webre, a hardworking country woman with the heaviest Cajun accent I've ever heard. What a time she had answering the office telephone!

She didn't say much, and what she did say wasn't easy to make out, if you didn't come from the same neck of the woods. But she worked hard to lighten up her accent. Dot never got to be much of a talker. Heck, if you didn't ask her anything she might go for days without making a sound, just going about her business. Still, she learned enough to become head of underwriting, which meant she screened all the applications, a job critical to the company's success.

After we sold Security Industrial in 1996, we formed the Ourso Management Company. And a few of the people who had been with me for many years continued to work for the new company. Cathy LeBlanc and Jesse Arboneaux are two of these.

Cathy is a person who's grown tremendously with the company by taking care of business. A student in the Cooperative Office Education (COE) program at Donaldsonville High School, she was working in an office next door to us when an opening occurred in our company. Cathy was just eighteen when she started in our office, in the beginning filing, typing, writing letters. She's still with us and I can tell you I'd be lost without her. Lord help me, but new technology has always puzzled me. How many times did I pound on the wall of my office, calling for help? Cathy has a saint's patience when it comes to helpful explanation of newfangled technology. She does what has to be done and takes the initiative to do it. When I say I'd be lost without her, I mean that just about literally, because she keeps my schedule of appointments and meetings, makes sure I'm where I need to be when I need to be there. Cathy's grown up, married, and reared a family, and in all this time has never once failed to complete an assignment. She does more than what's assigned. I've come to count on it.

That goes as well for Jesse Arboneaux, the management company's secretary and treasurer. He's in charge in the Donaldsonville office, where he and Cathy and Marlene, our office worker, hold down the fort. He came about the same time Cathy did. They're plainspoken, straightforward people.

Jesse began as an accountant, went to Nicholls State and got his MBA while working full time, and is now a crackerjack financial manager. For my money, he's the best in the business, which is why I trust a lot of it to his management. I don't know anyone with a better instinct for the management of funds. He's another person who has grown up through the company, while the company grew up around him.

Motivating, complimenting, building self-esteem

Many nights, during those years of growing, I lay awake in the dark, with my mind focused on motivating my employees, as it once focused on scrap paper and iron. How could I help these ordinary people achieve extraordinary things?

Sometimes I'd think up small reminders to keep them focused, to remind them of what they were capable of achieving. I bought cartons of tin cans and had white labels put on them with the words "Success

Two of my most valued and trusted employees, Jesse Arboneaux and Cathy LeBlanc, continued to work for me in my management company after I sold Security Industrial in 1996. Jesse is a top-flight financial manager with a keen instinct for managing funds and determining the value of businesses. Cathy is an administrative assistant who routinely goes above and beyond the call of duty in whatever task she is assigned.

That's me at right congratulating Dan Esquivel on a job well done – as usual! He was a highly productive district sales manager. A man of many talents, he was with the company for 36 years.

– Photography by Olan Mills

Irene Giroir of Houma was an ordinary woman who accomplished extraordinary things as a sales agent and sales manager for our company. Though she didn't have a formal education, she was highly effective in her work because of a strong native intelligence, keen problem-solving ability, and an uncanny talent for memorizing things.

John and Louise Fritz attending one of Security Industrial's annual company trips. A man with an extraordinarily sharp intellect, John played a key role in many of the acquisitions that built Security Industrial into a large and profitable company.

H.P. Williams was the most productive salesman in the history of Security Industrial Insurance Co. He out-sold every other agent practically every month for the entire 15 years he was with the company. A soft-spoken, likable fellow, he always carried his rate book with him in his suit pocket – so he'd be ready to sell a policy if he came upon an opportunity to make a sale. Talk about a salesman!

In her capacity as head of Security Industrial's underwriting department, Dorothy Weber screened all applications for insurance. A quiet, hardworking soul, she could go about her business for days without saying a word.

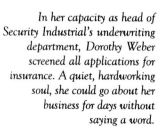

Sidney Harp grew up in and with the company, starting out as a bookkeeper, then moving to agent, staff manager, district manager, regional manager, and finally agency director. He was with the company 26 years, until it was sold.

Alvin Richard, Security's first bookkeeper, worked for the company the entire time I owned it – 48 years. He was instrumental in the acquisition of small companies in the early years of the business.

That's me seated in the background, worn out after helping pack 75 Thanksgiving food baskets for the less fortunate of Donaldsonville. This was a holiday tradition Margy and I enjoyed each Christmas and Thanksgiving for many years.

Sister Lillian McCormack of St. Michael Special School for exceptional children in New Orleans introduces me at a luncheon. St. Michael's is one of the charitable institutions Margy and I supported.

Photo courtesy of Kurt Coste and Children's Hospital of New Orleans

I enjoyed meeting 14-year-old Nicaraguan cardiac patient Augustin Flores-Morales and was glad to help with the medical expenses incurred following his open-heart surgery. He was a very polite young man, and very grateful. Children's Hospital of New Orleans and a team of surgeons donated their services. Augustin was in danger of "sudden death" due to a congenital heart disease. The surgery did save his life.

Internationally renowned Chef John Folse of Donaldsonville is one the young entrepreneurs I advised and worked with when he was just getting started in business.

Comes In Cans, Not In Cannots." I gave people plaques to hang on their walls with words of inspiration about excellence by Vince Lombardi. On my office wall, in front of my old school teacher's desk, I hung a sign that said "Think." I provided all our regional and district managers with similar signs.

A favorite motivational tool was the annual "Progress" walk. "Progress" was a mule, a jackass, from one of the farms near Donaldsonville. In fact, as the years went by there were several mules, but we called them all "Progress." Each year I made an agreement with our agency director, who had overall charge of our sales effort, that if the company met or exceeded its annual sales objective, I would lead "Progress" around Donaldsonville's downtown streets. If the company didn't meet its objective, the agency director got to take the walk with "Progress." I can tell you, I didn't mind the walk a bit. All of our employees and many of the townspeople turned out to cheer me on.

"Progress" enjoyed the day in town, a welcome break from his duties on the farm. Over the years the mules and I got to be close friends. I named the company newsletter after them: *Security Progress*.

Small gestures of recognition and appreciation are always important. Small gestures repeated add up to big gestures. For example, I made a point of personally signing the paychecks of our sales people. And I always wrote encouraging words on the check stubs – always in green ink, which employees came to regard as my trademark.

"Congratulations. You've sold $400 of insurance this week. Top $500 next week," I'd write.

Each time they'd reach a goal, I'd congratulate them and urge them to reach higher. I tried to show people they had the ability to succeed, show them they could succeed, and reward them for it. "Success Comes In Cans." The more successful they were the more their self-esteem grew; the more their self-esteem grew the more successful they became. It compounded exactly like compound interest.

There are some old-timers, now retired, around Donaldsonville who still have their check stubs – a thick record of their own growth and progress in life – some of which they carry around in worn, misshapen wallets. When I see them, they reach back, pull out their wallets, and extract these old check stubs, faded but legible, and show them to me to recall the old days, and their accomplishments. I smile and congratulate them again.

The most powerful single motivator was our annual company trip. Sales seminars, we called them. We went all over the country – Galveston, Miami Beach, Atlanta, Las Vegas. Once we went to Mexico City and once to Toronto.

We invited the top ten percent of our sales agents, as well as outstanding staff, district managers and regional managers, and put them all up at Caesar's Palace, or whatever the comparable hotel was where we were. The trip to Las Vegas was the most highly prized, maybe because it was the most lavish of cities. We returned there half a dozen times.

We'd rent one of the big convention rooms for our employee-recognition banquet. Agents who sold a certain amount of insurance or increased sales by a certain percentage throughout the year were invited, spouses included. Inviting the spouses doubled the production of self-esteem. Not only did the employee's self-esteem get a big boost but so did the spouse's. As I've said, success isn't a solo flight.

Security Industrial paid for the whole works, which included staying in the hotel in a king-sized room with all the trimmings. And suppose an agent double-qualified? Well, then that agent got to bring along another couple. Think of what this did for the self-esteem of the agents. They loved it, and Margy and I did, too.

You can bet Mary Horton and her agents loved these trips. They were professionals now, their Houma bartending days far behind them. They always went out and bought themselves expensive dresses, which they could now afford, for the yearly occasion. You could tell from the way these women dressed and conducted themselves that they thought of themselves as professionals.

Nobody enjoyed the yearly trips more than H.P. He and his wife, Amelia, usually brought two other couples with them. Imagine the great treasure of self-esteem and confidence H.P. and Amelia built up over the years.

On the night of the employee-recognition banquet, I served as master of ceremonies. Lord help me, standing up there with Margy at my side gave my own self-esteem a tremendous boost. I wouldn't have traded it for anything. I'd boom out over the microphone:

"Folks, Margy and I want to welcome all of you. We want to congratulate all of you — and that includes all you wives and husbands out there — for what you've all done this year. It's been a hell of a great year for Security Industrial.

"Well, guess what. H.P.'s our top dog again. I want you all to meet H.P. and Amelia Williams. Please stand up H.P. and Amelia."

And then H.P. and Amelia would slowly push back their chairs and rise to their feet, hands resting on the table, Amelia with a shy smile, shaking her head in mock disbelief.

"H.P.," I'd say. "H.P., you got your rate book with you?"

And H.P. would grin and would reach in his suit jacket's inside pocket and take out his old tattered and worn rate book and wave it over his head.

"Yes, sir," he'd say. "I got it right here. You need me to quote you a rate, Mr. Ourso?"

Amelia would slap him on the shoulder and whisper, so everybody could hear.

"H.P. hush," she'd say.

Everybody would cheer. And then I'd invite H.P. and Amelia up on stage with me. He was a slight man of medium height and very modest appearance, but you could tell as he approached the stage that his self-esteem was skyrocketing.

I never talked to our people much about money. Money itself was never the motivator. I talked to them about the good life that was possible if one worked hard. I talked to them about better houses, better neighborhoods in which to raise their kids, better schools and colleges for their children. I talked about how through hard work a person could improve the quality of his or her life. I said these things in the belief that the quality of life a person achieved had a lot to do with his or her self-esteem.

But, let me tell you this. The quality of life they achieved and the self-esteem they acquired as a result of that achievement had everything to do with my own self-esteem. Oh, mine had been on the boxing ring's canvas at LSU, and cold and low in my mule pack days, and it had taken a beating the day the State Insurance Commissioner wanted to close us down, and later when I found my policies impaled upon my clients' picket fences. But each time it got knocked down it got up, and little by little it recovered and grew over the years as Security Industrial grew and prospered.

I think this is why it always made sense to me to try to reward people as they deserved to be rewarded. If you don't pay people what they're worth, you lower their self-esteem, and in my view, your own as well. You can't hope to have a company of overperformers if you underpay them. As I've said, you need big people.

In nearly a half century Security Industrial Insurance Company acquired fifty-six other companies. That's more than one acquisition a year, though most of that growth occurred in the seventies and eighties.

We grew in all ways: in revenues, in profits, in the number of our employees. Our growth accelerated more and more, mostly because of the tremendous growth of the people themselves. The company grew internally as the employees, individually and collectively, grew, as their lives and their families increased. And I myself grew in self-esteem and confidence as the company did, so that the company's growth paralleled my own growth. Margy and I had invested more than money in Security Industrial; we had invested ourselves. The company's growth produced our own.

The more it gave to us the more we were able to give to ourselves, our children, and the community of Donaldsonville. Just as our employees' self-esteem soared as they became more and more successful, as they were able to give more and more to the people they served, so our self-esteem, Margy's and mine, soared as we were able to give more and more. Indeed, our sense of self-worth was tied directly to the worth of our company.

So, this is why, when it came time to part with the company in which we had invested so much of ourselves, it seemed so important that we get full and fair compensation. The people who thought we were crazy for not accepting the first offer, valued at $160 million, didn't understand that it was a chunk of ourselves we were parting with. And after all we had put into it, we did not want it to be undervalued. This wasn't just a money issue. It had to do with self-esteem as much as anything.

I have told you what a boost being a member of the Young Presidents Organization gave to my self-esteem. During the years I returned to the Harvard seminars my confidence grew. No more debate about what to do with old Ourso and his strange Cajun accent. No, now it was my choice.

"Ous, you want to lead off? Or conclude?" they'd ask me.

I liked the middle of the order just fine.

In the early days, when I told people I was from Donaldsonville, I said it with some trepidation.

"I'm just a country boy from Donaldsonville, Louisiana" meant exactly that. But over the years, as Security Industrial got on the map, climbed to the top of A.M. *Best's* list, and spread through Louisiana, the phrase gradually took on a different meaning. What I meant was this:

"Look, if this country boy from Donaldsonville, Louisiana, can succeed in what nobody except he himself thought could be done, with a bunch of plain country folks like himself, well then just think what you can do. Think about what's possible."

On our road to success, there were always plenty of people who doubted we would reach the goals to which we aspired. To them, I can only offer a piece of friendly advice:

"Success Comes In Cans, Not In Cannots."

CHAPTER 6

Doing For Others

SINCE WE WERE CHILDREN, MARGY AND I HAVE BEEN in the habit of doing for others, in one form or another. In rural communities such as Donaldsonville and White Castle doing for others is as natural as breathing. We all have an obligation to the people who have reared, nurtured and educated us. Where Margy and I come from, nobody goes it alone.

For me, it started small: I'd put a little of the money I earned from collecting scrap newspaper and iron into the collection plate at church. Later Margy and I tithed twenty-five dollars from my monthly salary of two hundred fifty. As I got raises, the first raise payment went to the church. When we had more, we started a private foundation to help the needy. Along the way we gave food to food drives, especially around Thanksgiving and Christmas.

Where we come from, this is what people do.

Tithing became a habit, part of the practice of our faith. I saw my father put the green bills in the offering plate each Sunday, the wad of bills growing or diminishing, signaling the family's rising or falling fortunes. Always there was something, no matter how hard the times. If money was impossible to come by, there was service, the giving of oneself. Margy and I didn't deliberately decide to tithe or render service; we did it, as had our parents before us, out of long-standing habit in our families.

Sometimes we heard about someone needing help. I gave Dan

Esquivel, one of my most trusted employees, five hundred dollars to take to a family of Mexican immigrants newly arrived in Donaldsonville. They needed clothes. Dan took the woman and her children shopping.

The giving grew as we grew. It grew to be part of everything we did. We bought a new school bus for Ascension Catholic High School, donated a million dollars to the New Orleans Archdiocese of the Catholic Church, distributed checks of five hundred dollars each to the parish priests in our immediate area, invited all the nuns from the high school to a Christmas luncheon.

We gave, mindful that our own good fortune did not come from our efforts alone. In appreciation of our support of the church and those who serve in it, the Archdiocese gave me a St. Louis Medallion; later, with papal approval, Archbishops Hannan and Schulte dubbed me a Knight of St. Gregory. After we sold Security Industrial, Margy and I were able to give LSU's College of Business Administration a fifteen million dollar endowment.

Of course, there were tax advantages in this, as my California friend Jack Anderson pointed out. I read an article about how Jack, a Harvard MBA, gave a large endowment to UCLA. But taxes weren't the reason for the gift. All the years since I'd left LSU, having not earned that letter jacket, I kept it in the back of my mind to return to the university some day and prove myself worthy. Also, I'd always wanted to do something that would make good education available to students in Louisiana who couldn't afford to attend top schools up East.

The endowment meant the college would be able to attract some of the best scholars and teachers in the country. With the sale of our company we were able to give to the college an endowment that would in perpetuity contribute to the quality of the education young men and women would receive there. Subsequently, the LSU Board of Supervisors re-named the business school the E.J. Ourso College of Business Administration. And the college established the Margy B. Ourso Excellence in Teaching Institute. The knowledge of this is a great reward and comfort to us.

The more successful you are the greater the obligation you have to do for others. To have been blessed with success, as Margy and I have been, means we can do more for the people who cared for us, even for strangers in need. In giving and doing for others we are acknowledging the Providential care we've received and the Providential nature of our success.

To fail in this acknowledgment would be arrogant. Do we think we accumulated all we have on our own? No, and we thank God for the abundance He has given us. We give in return, though we can't outdo His generosity. You've got to be generous, because you've got to know that no matter how much education, clout, or influence you have, you've had generous help from above.

So, when I'm asked about the ingredients of our success, one thing I say is that doing for others has been both vocation and avocation, by which I mean that it has been our way of doing business.

The more good you do for others the better you do for yourself. And the better you do for yourself, the more good you can do for others. Every day teaches me this simple truth.

Supporting poor, unwed mothers

In 1995, the year before Margy and I moved to New Orleans, a nurse came to our house in Donaldsonville to care for me as I convalesced from an illness. A pleasant-looking woman in her mid forties, she had the sturdy look of a person who was used to the long hours and the hard work of caring for others.

On her first day in our house, while she was waiting to meet me, she read some newspaper clippings about funeral homes we'd acquired down through the years. The clippings had been sitting out on an end table next to her chair. I sent for her, and she came up to the front of the house and stood before me in our living room, where I was sitting in front of the opened windows enjoying the view of our yard. This was in the late fall of the year, and the morning sunlight was streaming in through the French doors. The slight chill in the air felt healing.

The nurse introduced herself, and we exchanged pleasantries.

"Did you own Tharp-Sontheimer Funeral Home on Rampart Street in New Orleans?" she asked.

"Yes, for fourteen years I owned it," I replied.

"Eight years ago in New Orleans I gave birth to a stillborn child. The nurses at the hospital told me that Tharp-Sontheimer, owned by a Mr. Ourso, would bury the child, free. And if you wanted a service or a showing or presentation, they'd do that too, free. And they did it, free," the nurse recalled. "I never sent you a card, or thanked you in any way. So, I want to thank you for what you did for me eight years ago."

Her freshly starched white uniform gleamed in the sunlight.

"It was at Baptist Hospital in New Orleans. We never actually met, but even so you showed me a kindness that I have never forgotten. I was a young girl, unmarried, poor, and in my eighth month of pregnancy," she added.

One of our funeral homes had provided a casket and made provisions to have the poor infant properly buried.

"I have never forgotten that kindness to a poor girl who thought she didn't have a friend in the world," she said. "And I am pleased and grateful to be able to say thank you in person."

She did a little curtsey and went about her duties.

She recalled for me what I had not thought about for a long time. For many years, we made it a practice to provide funerals for stillborn infants whose parents were poor and unable to do so. We provided a small, white casket, secured the necessary permits, and gave other services connected with the burial, without asking for payment.

It turned out to be a service much needed and appreciated, since young, unmarried girls were often financially or emotionally unprepared to deal with the exigencies of a funeral. Among such poor girls, sometimes abandoned by their disapproving and unsympathetic families, commonly there had been inadequate prenatal care, which increased the likelihood of infant mortality. We saw this as a chance to do much good at no great expense. So I instructed our funeral homes, especially in urban areas, to inform hospitals of our willingness to do this.

Over the years the high infant death rate among the urban poor increased this expense, but we bore it as long as we could, until it became overwhelming. It was the practice of many of our funeral homes not only in New Orleans but throughout the state.

My nurse had been one of these poor girls, with no one to turn to in a time of sorrow and need, and we had been fortunate enough to be there for her. She carried her gratitude locked within her, waiting all these years, until that day in Donaldsonville when she was finally able to say thank you. She showed great kindness in the care she gave me during my convalescence. Her expression of appreciation added its healing powers to those of the fall sun and air.

Giving Chef John Folse a boost

When Professor Bob Justis brings his MBA students to talk with me, they always ask about success in business. And I always tell them that giving to others, doing for other people, was a critical ingredient in the success of Security Industrial.

Students in colleges of business are routinely taught that the obligation of the business person is to make more and more profit, as long as the rules of the game are observed. Milton Friedman said this to the YPOers at Harvard. But I tell these LSU students success is a community effort. That's why I try to do as much as I can for young entrepreneurs, especially here in Louisiana.

When Chef John Folse was starting out in Donaldsonville, I did what I could to help him. Now he has an international reputation in Cajun cuisine.

In the beginning it was very different. Margy and I would go over to LaFitte's Landing for dinner on a Saturday evening. The parking lot would be nearly empty. Inside, you'd go snow-blind from white tablecloths at empty tables.

"Margy," I'd say, "next time remind me to bring my sunglasses!"

I'd have a martini with John. He'd laugh at my joke about the sunglasses, but the wolf was at his door.

At that time, the food writers were all over Paul Prudhomme down in New Orleans. Cajun and Creole food was as hot as a firecracker. People came from all over the country to K-Paul's Restaurant.

I set my martini down on the bar and turned to John.

"What's the difference here? What have you got? What have you got that those food writers haven't seen?" I asked him.

John looked dubious. I went on:

"Well, you're in a building built in the 1700s, before the Revolution. You've got real swamps and bayous nearby. Plantation houses all over the place. If those writers knew what you've got here, they'd be writing up a storm."

Sure, but how was he going to get all those writers from up East, in Boston and New York and Philadelphia, and the ones in Chicago and St. Louis and Atlanta to come to Donaldsonville to see what he had? I told John that if he could find a way to get them here, I'd help him put on a show they wouldn't soon forget.

Already my mind was racing ahead, dreaming up all sorts of tours with country breakfasts and lavish dinners cooked by John in authentic plantation kitchens and served in authentic plantation dining rooms. I'd supply the limousines.

No more than a week later John was in my office, grinning up at those framed buzzards hanging on my wall. He was excited. He'd been in Baton Rouge for a travel writers' luncheon sponsored by the Baton Rouge Convention & Visitors Bureau. These people came from all over the country. John couldn't wait for the meal to be done. He rushed up to the director of the tourism bureau.

"How'd you do it? How'd you get all these writers down here?" he asked.

Well, he had enlisted the help of airlines and bus companies, and in the interest of promoting travel and commerce, they provided transportation free of charge. Moreover, the writers had been wined and dined all over at no cost to themselves or to the news media they represented.

That very afternoon, John and I mapped out a four-day food tour of the bayou country, with a grand finale at his restaurant, of course. Once they got down here – and you better believe they were eager to take us up on the free lunch – I had them driven all over the area in limousines. We had them meet the mayors of Donaldsonville and Baton Rouge and the Governor of Louisiana himself.

It was a tremendous success. We focused on Louisiana, but as soon as they got back to their newspapers and magazines they wrote all about Chef John Folse and LaFitte's Landing and the wonderful food he had provided. The response was substantial and immediate. People began to show up at John's restaurant. The parking lot filled up with cars with license plates from many states. John was getting national attention.

And he got international attention shortly thereafter when he went to the Soviet Union to cook at the opening of a restaurant in Moscow, one of the first U.S.-Soviet joint ventures. It happened to coincide with the Reagan-Gorbachev summit. The Russians gave John a medal.

Members of the press from more than a dozen countries attended the opening of the restaurant. ABC and CNN covered it. When it was time to come home John invited the Russians to bring ten chefs to the United States for a ten-day coast-to-coast tour. Another newsmaker: one of the first Soviet-American culinary exchanges.

When John got back from Moscow, he and I sat down and drew up a list of companies whose help we would solicit. Delta would provide air travel to JFK Airport. The Culinary Institute of America was involved. From New York the ten Russian chefs were flown to Chicago, where they toured meat-packing facilities, watched the cutting of thick steaks. They went to Atlanta and toured CNN, and then on to Disneyland in time to be served some of Walt Disney's birthday cake. They stayed at the Marriott in New Orleans, visited catfish farms in Mississippi, went to Dallas, Colorado and Los Angeles. John wrapped it up with a fabulous dinner prepared by him. Of course, the large press *entourage* that went along closely observed and reported all of this.

In the small, rural communities in which Margy and I grew up, caring for others meant that others would care for you when you needed it. You kept an eye out for them, and they kept an eye out for you. Success came through community effort.

Providing for people in need meant that when the time came these people, or others who had heard of your kindnesses, would reciprocate and provide for you.

In the early years our business did not have money for public relations or advertising. Giving, helping, doing for others was our public relations program. And believe me, it paid off, financially and in other ways.

Compared to other businesses, that of providing funeral services and related merchandise offers unique opportunities to do for others. I once read in *The Times Picayune* about the death of an old and notable jazz musician, a black man who had so long outlived members of his family that no one came forward to provide the funeral and burial that a man of his accomplishment deserved.

He had died poor and all but forgotten, until someone at the newspaper realized who he was and how important and influential he had been in his day. Right after I read this story I called the newspaper for the details of the musician's situation. I told them I would be honored if we could make arrangements for his funeral and burial, which we did without charge.

We did it first rate. And you wouldn't believe how many people showed up for the services, once they knew who this man was and how important his influence had been for so many musicians who came after him. It was a great opportunity to do something for someone who had touched more lives than he knew.

I think that's the way life is: What you do will certainly touch more lives than you know. Like dropping a stone in a pond, doing good sends ripples beyond your view.

Searching out Social Security beneficiaries

Some years after the end of World War II I saw great opportunity in the large number of people who were entitled to Social Security benefits but – because of illiteracy or lack of education – were unaware of what was rightly theirs. They had no idea of what they were entitled to.

Here was a tremendous opportunity to help these people receive the benefits they should have been getting. Security Industrial helped thousands of people get this unanticipated financial assistance.

How did I discover this great opportunity? Simply by opening my eyes to the near-at-hand. One day I read a newspaper article in the *Donaldsonville Chief* about a young woman whose husband had drowned in a boating accident. The young woman, expecting their first child, was left destitute, without means of support. Her husband had recently returned home after four years in the U.S. Marine Corps, during which he distinguished himself for bravery in the Pacific Campaign.

Now, how could the wife of such a distinguished veteran be left so destitute? I knew veterans were entitled to Social Security benefits by virtue of their service in the armed forces. Though we had not handled the family's funeral arrangements, I went to talk to the young woman's father-in-law. I wanted to tell him about the benefits to which his daughter-in-law and her child, his grandchild, were entitled and to get information that would allow me to fill out the necessary forms to help them. But the man was hostile, would not let me in the house. He refused to speak with me.

"Please leave, and leave us alone," he said. He stood blocking the doorway.

I asked to speak with his daughter-in-law. No, that was not possible either, since she had gone off to Georgia, presumably to have her child. The father-in-law, moreover, wanted nothing to do with her; he hoped he had seen the last of her. He had not favored the marriage to begin with and now, irrationally, he held her responsible for his son's death. As for me, he suspected I was soliciting business and intended to take advantage of him and his family in their grief.

"Just leave, and don't come back," he said as he shook his fist.

I left and went about locating the Marine's brothers and other members of the family, in the hope that they would be more cooperative and would find the widow in Georgia. They were indeed cooperative. They supplied the information I needed to fill out the forms on her behalf, but they didn't know where she was. She had gone off alone to have her child, leaving no forwarding address.

It took the Social Security people twelve years to find her. The child, a girl, was by then in junior high school, but the mother and daughter were given the accumulated benefits for those twelve years. They would continue to receive these benefits until the girl reached twenty-two, provided she stayed in school. The mother wrote, thanking me for my effort. Her large childlike handwriting was on lined notebook paper, probably from the daughter's school tablet. She said it was money from heaven.

During those twelve years – each of which I filled out and sent in the Social Security forms – I learned a great deal about Social Security and the huge number of people entitled to its benefits who nevertheless did not receive them. There were literally thousands of people near at hand who never received the benefits they were entitled to simply because they did not know they were entitled. Many of them couldn't fill out the forms. Many, who spoke French and little English, couldn't read enough to learn about Social Security.

We took advantage of the opportunity to help these people. I carried the Social Security forms with me to the homes of the bereaved families and included filling out the forms for those who couldn't do this for themselves as a part of the services we provided. We never charged for this. I sat at the family's kitchen table – perhaps one of the same kitchen tables at which I'd sat years before talking to a young wife about burial insurance – and took down the information for the form. Our secretary typed up the forms, and we sent them in on behalf of the widow.

Meanwhile, I followed the bureaucratic developments of Social Security, immersed myself in Social Security administration and procedure, sat up in bed reading into the night, and eventually became so informed that lawyers sent their clients to me for help. For many, these Social Security benefits were like manna from heaven, a Godsend that enabled widows to raise and educate their children. This was especially important for widows left with the large families typical of this part of Louisiana.

Some cases were more complex and challenging than others. A young, single girl had had a child by a bartender, who was killed in an automobile wreck soon after the child's birth. Because they were as yet unmarried, and maybe didn't even intend to marry, it appeared it was going to be difficult for this girl to get the benefits she would have been clearly entitled to had she and the bartender been married. However, the bartender had been friendly with a priest, who occasionally patronized the bar where he worked, and the bartender had confessed to the priest – as a friend rather than in the confessional – that he was the child's father. The priest, though he had not come to know this through the confessional, was reluctant to testify at a hearing before the Social Security Commission. What he knew he had learned in confidence. We petitioned the commission on the young mother's behalf. The commission granted benefits for the young mother and her daughter, even without a hearing, though this is very unusual in cases where paternity can be questioned.

Italian widows were most likely to need this service. Since immi-grants and even the sons of immigrants often had trouble finding em-ployment, Italian men were likely to be self-employed. Denied – as was the great A.P. Giannini – the usual routes to employment, they went into business for themselves. The bias against immigrant groups forced them to be entrepreneurs. The widows often did not have their de-ceased husbands' Social Security numbers, but even so we were able to get them benefits. It might be only $32 a month, but back then that was a more considerable sum than it is now.

Soon we became widely known to Italian communities. People came to us from miles around. Sometimes we had to appeal a case; some-times we had to write to Washington. But we always secured the ben-efits. Some Saturdays we had four secretaries hard at work typing Social Security forms. The line of people waiting for help was longer than we had anticipated. We worked into the evening, if that's what it took, rather than turn anyone away.

Lord, talk about public relations! I don't think any amount of money could have purchased the public relations benefits we received from our efforts simply to care for these people.

Doing for others, Donaldsonville-style

When I was at Harvard with all those successful people, I felt the business I was in was less than flashy. Selling burial insurance and managing funeral homes didn't have the glitter of computer chips. It wasn't BIC pens. But it was a business that involved taking care of people, of providing for people, doing for them what they could not at that moment do for themselves.

As Security Industrial grew over the years, one of the great rewards for Margy and me was that we were more and more able to do for other people, for our relatives and our neighbors, and for the larger commu-nities embraced by our church and our state.

In Donaldsonville, doing for other people often meant giving food. When it comes to individuals, person-to-person giving, I've come to prefer giving food. I liked to go to 4-H Fairs and buy hogs or steers or poultry. I'd have them properly butchered and packaged and then give them away to families in need.

In Donaldsonville, holidays, such as Halloween, Thanksgiving, Christ-mas and Easter, were occasions that involved giving food. For Hallow-een, when our children were children, we went all out. I'd set up a long table on the sidewalk in front of our house and lay out baskets of all sorts of candy and treats: Hershey bars, licorice, apples on sticks, or-anges, Baby Ruths, and tons of candy corn.

Every child in Donaldsonville costumed as witch, cowboy, monster or ghost showed up at our house with a brown paper bag. They held out the bags and waited patiently for us to drop treats into them, not moving on to the next house until their bags were ready to burst. They walked for miles to get to our house because they'd heard about us. Can't beat word-of-mouth advertising.

Our own children loved it. We all dressed in costumes for the occasion, Margy as an angel, I as a pirate.

Thanksgiving, Margy and I prepared baskets of food for poor people who couldn't afford the traditional turkey dinner. I don't know how many baskets we made up, but Margy and I and the children worked on them for the whole week before Thanksgiving Day, packing in the turkey and all the trimmings – canned cranberries, pumpkin pies, yams.

Then we'd turn around and do the same thing for Christmas, except then we might include a smoked ham or a goose. The day before Thanksgiving or Christmas, our office people and agents went out, their automobiles loaded with the baskets. They always returned with tales of how pleased people were to receive these gifts. It made our people feel good to be a part of this. In fact, they were a very important part of it, because this bounty flowed from the collective efforts of all the employees of Security Industrial. Without their conscientious work we couldn't have succeeded to the extent that we did.

For Christmas we had the Nuns' Luncheon. It began as a luncheon the week before Christmas each year, or sometimes as late as early January, at the Village Restaurant in Baton Rouge, for the community of nuns who taught at Ascension Catholic High School in Donaldsonville. Margy and I sent each sister an invitation. But word got around and our invitation list grew to include guests who might happen to be at the convent at that time, perhaps having been transferred back from duty in Japan or Puerto Rico.

It grew so large we decided to go to Antoine's in New Orleans, where we rented the Rex Room. One of the elderly nuns resisted this move, fearing that Antoine's would not have oysters, which were her favorite dish. But, of course, her fear was unfounded: Antoine's has thirty different kinds of oysters – and she ate so many that her stomach hurt.

I swear, it got so that nuns from orders all over the country contrived to be in Donaldsonville or New Orleans around Christmastime. They loved Antoine's with its glittering crystal chandeliers, its walls covered with the pictures of famous people and events and souvenirs. We invited not only the nuns but some of the brothers as well. What a feast it got to be! I loved it as much as any of them.

But not all of our dealings with the nuns were of a festive nature. Back in the mid- to late-1980s we learned of a huge financial problem being borne by religious sisters and brothers: a multi-billion dollar shortage of funds to care for aged and infirm members of various religious orders throughout the nation.

It was quite distressing to me to realize that these religious people – who had spent their entire adult lives educating, encouraging and counseling others in need (including me) – were now in need of support themselves, but the money simply was not there to adequately fund their retirement and medical needs. In fact, a comprehensive nation-wide survey of religious orders concluded that the shortfall was $2.5 billion and growing. A staggering amount by any standard.

While the National Conference of Catholic Bishops and others grappled with the problem at the national level, I went to see my old friend, Fr. Philip Hannan, who was now Archbishop of the Archdiocese of New Orleans, to see what could be done locally, in our own backyard. Together, along with a sister and brother, we established a foundation – the Catholic Aged Religious Endowment (CARE), a mechanism designed to help fund these needs in the New Orleans area.

Margy and I donated $100,000 to get it started, and another donor gave an old building in downtown New Orleans that was later sold, with proceeds going to the foundation. Various fundraising projects added to the bank account during the twelve years that the foundation was active. In 1999 the balance of the fund was given to a local retirement home for aged religious brothers and sisters.

The grand *boucherie*

Of all the festive occasions Security Industrial was involved in, the biggest was our annual Donaldsonville *boucherie*. Margy and I invited relatives, friends and neighbors, as well as bankers and other business associates from New Orleans and Baton Rouge and as far away as Atlanta and New York. We did this every year for fifteen years, until we were feeding two or three hundred people.

We started preparations for the *boucherie* three weeks in advance. Margy and I did much of the work, but once we got going everybody pitched in. Family, the neighbors, everybody was welcome to help. The work took place on long tables set out in our backyard, turning it into a great big outdoor kitchen.

Boucherie literally means butchering; in south Louisiana it refers to the killing and butchering of a hog. We usually got six hogs. I'd go to the country outside of Donaldsonville, to one of the farmers who raised hogs, and ask him to set aside six for us and to put them on corn and water. My grandfather had told me two weeks of this diet would make the meat especially flavorful.

"Feed your pig garbage, and he'll taste like garbage. Corn-fed hogs are best," he used to say.

The farmer butchered the hogs and brought them in his pickup truck.

No part of the hog went unused. We put the feet in a large iron pot and slowly cooked them down to a gelatin, which we used as an ingredient in making hog's head cheese. There was backbone stew, salt meat from the forelegs, and cracklins from the skin. We stuffed the stomach with cornbread and baked it. We boiled the large intestines overnight for the chitlins, dipped them in cornmeal and egg and fried them in strips an inch and a quarter wide. The smell hung in the live oaks' low limbs. Of course, there was also smoked ham. We didn't throw away so much as a scrap.

Seems like no one declined our invitation to the *boucherie*. They all came, more and more each year, and many brought guests, until the crowd swelled to three hundred, maybe more. I didn't count; I was too busy with the cooking and stirring and serving.

The day of the feast we always had two bands, a black jazz band and a Cajun band. They set up in the middle of the yard and took turns playing thirty-minute sets. The jazz band played traditional New Orleans jazz favorites: "Way Down Yonder in New Orleans" and "When the Saints Go Marching In."

One of our agents, Pat David from Rayne, played with the Cajun band, whose members came from the French-speaking country around Lafayette. They liked the audience to sing along. Their lead singer would sing a few lines, then all the people would shout, "*Et là-bas, Et là-bas*" and "*Aiyee.*" They never tired of it. "*Et là-bas, Et là-bas.*"

The *boucherie* started around five in the afternoon and went on until all the food was gone. The cracklins' aroma drew our guests to the tables. But everyone's favorite was the pig's tail and turnips. Our guests would eat, then dance and drink – and eat and dance and eat some more. Eventually, every scrap was devoured.

Each year more and more people came. An invited guest might show up with twenty-two guests of his own in tow. What could we say? It was exhausting, but Margy and I loved to have people come over and have a good time, so we kept it up as long as we could.

In May of 1996 Louisiana State University awarded me an honorary Doctorate in Humane Letters. The speaker making the presentation, Dean Tom Clark of the College of Business Administration, told the graduates and their parents that the degree was awarded in recognition of my entrepreneurial accomplishments and contributions to the state of Louisiana.

His speech turned my face a shade of red, hearing the nice things he said about me. Still, I couldn't help but remember my shame at Coach Khoury's answer to my question about getting one of those coveted LSU letter jackets. Here I was, back at LSU, at last found worthy.

For Margy and me, the occasion was one of our proudest moments. I was at long last receiving an LSU degree, which I had desired for so many years. It took a while, but here it was, now being placed in my hand in the purple and gold case, and draped over my shoulders in the form of the purple and gold doctoral hood.

The dean asked me to say a few words to the graduates. It's always been difficult for me, in front of such an audience, to say just a few words. But I did my best. I grasped the podium with all the energy I could muster.

"You can't just be a Fighting Tiger in the football stadium. You've got to show them in your life. If an ex-chicken salesman can do it, so can you," I said.

I tried to convey to them what life has taught me: You have obligations to the people, communities, institutions and Supreme Being who have nurtured you, and these obligations go on throughout your life. It begins in the beginning and it doesn't stop until those six carry you out.

These few words set my personal record for brevity, but they reflected one of the most important lessons life has taught me.

CHAPTER 7

Growth Through Acquisitions

I F I'VE BEEN ASKED ONCE, I'VE BEEN ASKED A
hundred times: What are the principles of wealth acquisition? Some
people think I have a secret I can reveal. I wish I did, but I don't.
All I can say is that Margy and I accumulated the wealth we have day
by day, through patient effort. Each day we just tried to do a little bit
better than we'd done the day before. We tried to grow.

We attribute our success to compound interest, perseverance, a
Donaldsonville education, good country people who think out of the
box, and a huge helping of Divine Providence. Don't forget that. How
else do ordinary people do extraordinary things?

Those are the ingredients, but you combine them your own way. We
all have our own ways. Doing it our way was important to us. Had we
copied a recipe from someone else's cookbook for success, it wouldn't
have been Margy and me, and it wouldn't have worked.

In the beginning we had no clear idea where we were headed. We
were too busy surviving each week to look far ahead. At night I lay in
the dark thinking, *Where are we going to get money for Friday's payroll?* But
every week somehow we got it, as Margy always assured me we would.
Without Margy I couldn't have gotten from one week to the next.

There are people who inherit wealth. Not us, though Margy's folks
owned dry goods stores in several parts of Louisiana and lived in a big
house in White Castle. There are people who suddenly strike it rich,
like prospectors or people who win the lottery. That's not us either,

though we've certainly had more than our share of good luck. Nor are we among those people who come up with some new product or service that takes the market by storm, like Bill Gates and his computer programs.

We started out on the ladder's bottom rung and worked our way up, a rung at a time, one acquisition at a time. It was a slow climb and a long while before we got high enough up in that tree of wealth to get some good pickings.

Each day I woke up and told myself to do a little bit better. If I sold $1,000 worth of insurance last month, I tried for $1,500 this month. I focused on the next acquisition. At night I studied Giannini. The book on Giannini inspired me.

We stayed with what we knew – funeral homes and burial insurance – and worked on getting more of it. In my mind, I got the idea that we could get $1 billion of insurance in force. To try to achieve this goal Security Industrial grew and expanded internally and externally.

We grew internally by increasing productivity, which meant we all tried to sell a little more insurance each day than we had the day before, to increase the value of the assets we had. We each tried to grow. I woke up in the morning with my head filled with new ways to motivate people. I had them read books, go to meetings, take notes. I stressed listening.

"Listen, listen, listen to what people say," I told them. "Why do you think the good Lord gave us two ears but only one mouth?"

External growth came through acquisition of other companies or parts of companies. During the nearly half century we were in business, we made fifty-six acquisitions, mostly one at a time. No two were the same. Each had its own peculiarities. We acquired funeral homes, insurance companies, cemeteries, and a controlling interest in a limousine company.

But not one of all those fifty-six acquisitions was "by the book," unless you count Giannini's book, or Napoleon Hill's, or Russell Conwell's. Those were my books, not so much about acquisitions as about life.

Sure, "the book" – that is, the books assigned in business classes – tells you a lot you need to know about what the numbers mean. But that's not all you need to know. Each acquisition requires its own approach. For example, find out the key person to talk with, the person most influential in the decision. What are that person's interests? What does that person want? And you need to know how to talk with that person, what language to use – banker's, accountant's, lawyer's? You won't find those things in the book. Each person is unique. Each wants something different. You'd need a new book for each acquisition.

We didn't always win. Sometimes we didn't get the company we wanted or didn't get it right away.

One day I knocked on Geesey-Ferguson's door in Crowley. It was a nice little funeral home in a nice town. Sidney Harp was with me. We went in and sat in Mr. Ferguson's office.

"Mr. Ferguson," I said, "I'd like to buy your business."

"Get out and don't come back," he told me.

Wham! The door slammed shut behind us.

He was furious. Didn't even ask the amount of my offer. He wasn't going to part with his business, no matter what the price. Could I blame him? *Well, Mr. Ferguson,* I thought, *I might come back to see you in another year.* Things change. But they never did with Mr. Ferguson. He hung on to what was his. It wasn't big, but it was his. He'd poured his blood, sweat and tears into it. I understood that.

Sometimes we did all our homework and put in the best bid and still didn't get the company because of some circumstance we hadn't foreseen. That happened the summer after I'd gone to New York's Chase Manhattan Bank with Mike Schott, an MBA intern. We had done our homework: charts, graphs, tables. It takes nerve to march into Chase Manhattan and ask for $28 million.

We met with the loan committee for two hours over lunch. Those fellows asked us questions and more questions. A sharp group of young fellows. We spoke banker's talk. We got the loan alright, $28 million, but lost the bid for First National Life Insurance Co.

That really knocked us down. You get knocked down – you get the old taste of blood and canvas – and you get up and fight again.

Then some of the New Orleans funeral home crowd tried to keep us from doing business in the big city. But they couldn't keep us out. When somebody said to me, "You can't," I always thought, *I can.*

That New Orleans crowd didn't think we had what it took. But for us it was "Root hog or die! Drive like hell for Bastogne." We got a toehold, and then a beachhead, and then, hell, we won the Battle of the Bulge – or should I call it "The Battle for New Orleans."

Early acquisitions (1950-68)

We made our first acquisition in 1950, after we'd been in business just two years. We acquired two Donaldsonville debit routes from Rabenhorst Funeral Home of Baton Rouge for $20,000.

Rabenhorst may have figured these routes would be eroded by us anyway. So, why not sell them and get something for them? The remoteness of the routes from Baton Rouge made eventual loss very likely. And it was no trouble for us to pick them up; we were right there. So, we got the monthly premiums and Rabenhorst's reserve associated with the two debit routes. We paid the note with the premiums, so the acquisition cost us no money. The cream paid for the cow.

This was a small acquisition, not even a whole company, but it pointed the way to make acquisitions and grow without having cash on hand.

This was about the same time I first encountered Giannini. I said to myself, *If he can do it, why can't we?* I read that book over and over, and each time I saw something new.

We took a big step in 1952 with the acquisition of the Florida Parishes Service Insurance Company of Amite and East Louisiana Burial Insurance Company. Florida Parishes was owned by a woman who had two sons. They had 100 agents, mostly part-timers, who were collecting only $6,000 a month. I went over and held a meeting with all the company's employees.

"Give me three months to show you what Security Industrial can do for you," I told them.

I wanted to show them what it was to be on a winning team. We encouraged the part-timers to become full-time agents. I preached the benefits of playing full-time on a winning team. If you work hard your earnings will go up, up. No limit. Some hardworking salespeople make more than the company president, as in H.P. Williams' case, I pointed out. H.P. made so much as an agent he didn't want to be a manager. As for Florida Parishes, some took to it, some didn't. In three months we had fewer but better agents, who each day made deposits in local banks – which enhanced our company's visibility and credibility, as well as the agents' own self-esteem. People in the communities they lived and worked in got to know these agents as professionals in their field. The recognition gave them a boost.

We easily paid the notes on the acquisition with the increase in premium revenues. Again, we had grown with no money. We converted weekly collection routes to monthly collection, which meant the people in the field could spend more time selling. It was a small move, which made a big difference. All in all, we had managed to grow without increasing our expenses.

That same year, 1952, we purchased the East Louisiana Burial Insurance Company of Hammond, our first black-owned company. The family who owned East Louisiana had a place in Kentwood and also branches in Amite, Hammond and Ponchatoula.

The funeral home market has always been segmented along racial lines. White people get buried out of white homes, black people out of black homes. We didn't see why that meant Security Industrial should be made up of only white companies. The acquisition of East Louisiana, however, was controversial. Some white business people regarded it with suspicion. East Louisiana's black competitors spoke disparagingly of it. But both groups were wrong.

When we purchased it, East Louisiana was averaging $100 worth of collections per debit route per month. I made the same speech I'd made at Florida Parishes: Give me three months to show you what we can do. You want to be on a winning team? East Louisiana became a successful company.

A handful of ragtag men and women from Donaldsonville and then from Amite, Hammond and Ponchatoula, we aimed to become state champions.

In 1954 we acquired Fidelity Life & Casualty Company of New Iberia, which proved to be a lot of work because its debit routes were scattered all over the place.

In 1955 we picked up the Iberia Hospital Service Company. They were in bad shape, with just a few agents. We worked to turn that around. We were building a good reputation, which helped us to deal with the banks.

We got another New Iberia company, Teche Life Insurance Company, the same year, 1955. At the closing, I phoned Fidelity Bank and Trust in Baton Rouge and asked them to wire me $25,000. We needed it to make the purchase. The bank wired the money without blinking an eye.

In 1963 we purchased Acadia Life Insurance Company and Gossen Funeral Home of Rayne. In 1968 we acquired Jacquemoud Funeral Home, which was owned by directors of the First National Bank of New Iberia. They worked with us even though we didn't have an account with this bank. We converted the securities and bonds to cash and made a deposit.

Seventeen years before to the day, the State Commissioner of Insurance had called me in to close us down. We'd come far in the area of trust and credibility. Security Industrial was a company with a high reputation. People we didn't know knew us. They thought of us as the guys who acquired companies and turned them into successes.

A sticky situation in Bogalusa

During the 1960s Security Industrial acquired seventeen companies. Most years we had at least a couple of acquisitions. In 1959 we had a little more than $14 million of insurance in force. By 1970 we had nearly $80 million. We set our sights high: one billion dollars of insurance in force.

We piled up acquisitions, but they didn't all come easy. An acquisition could take a very long time, if you counted from the time we approached the owner and expressed interest. Months. Or years.

Poole Funeral Benefit Association of Bogalusa took me five years to acquire from my first visit to Bogalusa to see the elderly widow who owned it. We finally made the acquisition in 1962. May Poole, even at 78, was as shrewd a business person as any with whom I've dealt. Though I visited her regularly, she held out, wouldn't consider selling. After a while, I got to know her. She was likeable, but could be as stubborn as a mule.

To understand this acquisition you need to know about her son and daughter. The son was married, and just before taking a trip to Spain he made a will in which he left everything to his wife. He also gave her power of attorney. Following his return from Spain the son attempted to commit suicide. The attempt left him in a coma. Mrs. Poole was doubly distraught over the tragedy, not only because her son nearly died, but also because she was not particularly fond of her daughter-in-law, who would come to own her son's assets if he died.

Nor was Mrs. Poole fond of her son-in-law, who had lost a large inheritance on ill-advised investments in restaurants in Florida and Texas – and in an airplane to fly back and forth.

I could see that the widow was not anxious to let her business or its proceeds fall into the hands of her offspring's spouses. She didn't want her daughter-in-law to end up with the property; nor did she relish the thought of her son-in-law squandering the fruit of her deceased husband's life's work.

I used to go to her house just about every month, hoping she'd sell. She said she wasn't interested. She wouldn't let me in the door. For years I never got past the huge white Dorian columns on the front porch of her big Southern mansion. She was suspicious. She talked to me standing just outside her front door on her big white porch, her arms folded tightly across her narrow chest, wisps of grey hair floating about her face.

"Say what you have to say right where you are, Mr. Ourso, and be brief about it," she'd tell me.

Talk about a tough customer. Worse than an Army mule. In this way for years she had resisted the temptation to sell, despite the increasingly burdensome day-to-day tasks of running the business. But she was 78; she knew she needed to do something.

When I heard her son lay in a coma following a suicide attempt, I took her two dozen red roses. She came outside onto the porch as usual.

"I'm sorry about your son's tragedy," I said, holding the roses out toward her.

I hadn't intended to talk business with her at all, but those roses literally opened the door. For the first time she reached back and opened the door and beckoned to me to come into the house. She was touched by the roses.

"Why, Mr. Ourso, how kind of you, how kind."

She led the way through a large entrance hall. What a grand house it was, with huge, high-ceiling rooms furnished with heavy, dark furniture. We walked over beautifully carpeted floors, through rooms and rooms, each filled with a matched set of the heavy, elegant furniture. There was a hush about the house. Somewhere upstairs in a bedroom, her son lay in a coma.

She spoke in a whisper, rolling her pale eyes toward the top of the wide circular staircase as we passed, as if afraid to disturb him. She put the roses in a green glass vase.

"Aren't they beautiful," she said. There were no other flowers in the room.

We sat in big, dark leather chairs in her sitting room and talked about her son. She had had him brought back from the hospital into this big house. The daughter-in-law was here, too, though she did not appear. Together, it seemed, mother and wife tended to the son, shared the caring, though they cared little for one another. Still, Mrs. Poole was not above business that afternoon. She let me know she was at long last thinking about selling Poole's Benefit Association. Of course, she knew I was interested, and if my bid were acceptable, well...

I could see the simple roses had won great favor with her. But, mind you, I was not the only one to have approached her about selling. She directed me to her accountant and her lawyer, who were about to announce a request for bids, leading me to understand that they had charge of her business affairs.

At the door, I told her I hoped her son would soon recover his health. She seemed doubtful, but grateful for my concern and sympathy. She was shrewd and cagey, even in the midst of personal tragedy, but I liked her, and really did hope for her son's recovery.

That afternoon's hushed conversation with Mrs. Poole gave me a glimpse of a woman I hadn't suspected, beyond the hard-nosed businesswoman I'd taken her for. As we all do, she labored under the burdens of a life that had its trials and troubles. Her son's caretaker, she herself had need of care and consideration.

The widow's unexpected turn very much encouraged me. But I wondered, *Who were our competitors?* I needed to know who we were up against. Were they big outfits with a lot of cash? Where did they come from? If they were big, how would I be able to outbid them? As she had suggested, I went to see the accountant and the lawyer, both of whom were anxious for her to sell, especially the lawyer, who stood to receive a nice fee, especially if it were a cash deal. I had several talks with the lawyer, but gained very little knowledge of my competitors. I suspected they were big New Orleans outfits, which would mean they'd have the upper hand in a cash deal.

But all the companies we had acquired up until then we acquired with no cash. Till then the no-cash strategy wasn't merely an option, it was a necessity. Our cash was tied up in reserves, our surplus in long-term investments. We didn't have cash to spare. Could we hope to win here?

Well, you have to anticipate, to be prepared with a plan – or two. Remember General Patton? He had three plans in place when he walked into Eisenhower's staff meeting. Let the other generals laugh; he was ready to move. He succeeded where they dared not attempt.

Across the street from the lawyer's office in Bogalusa stood a men's boarding house with a big white front porch with rocking chairs for the residents. I noticed that each day a thin old man, obviously one of the residents, sat out on the porch and smoked. He sat there when I arrived and when I left, rocking gently, smoking, looking out over the porch rail at cars passing in the street. Occasionally he'd wave to me. He'd gotten to know who came and went. So one day, I waved back and walked across the street and introduced myself. His pale blue eyes took my measure, took in the details of my business suit and shoes. Unblinking through the smoke, he sized me up.

I told him I'd like to engage his help. It wasn't going to mean doing anything much more than what he was already doing, I assured him. He leaned forward in his chair. And exactly what *would* it mean. All he had to do was sit right here like he usually did and write down the license plate numbers of automobiles that come to the lawyer's office across the street. I gave him $20, a pad of paper, and a pencil and told him I'd give him another $20 when I came back for the numbers. Sure, what an easy way to earn $40. No questions about why I wanted this information. Three days later I came back and got the numbers from him, gave him another $20, and thanked him for his trouble.

A friend of mine worked for the State in Baton Rouge; he looked up the most frequently appearing numbers in the official records. I had been right. Two big New Orleans outfits were my competitors – not good news since they had lots of cash and would no doubt put in hefty bids.

But I didn't think cash was the name of this game.

By now it was bid day, and I had to act fast. I knew the accountant and the lawyer were to have lunch with Mrs. Poole, and I asked them to find out for me her disposition to a cash bid. They both assured me that she would want cash. I thought differently. She didn't want the son and daughter to some day suddenly come into all that money, and have it shortly thereafter fall into the hands of their respective spouses. No, she'd try to avoid that. She'd go for an arrangement that would allow her to continue living as she had but without the day-to-day burden of running the business. She had to care for her stricken son.

The lawyer came back from lunch and reported what the widow had said:

"Heck no, I don't want cash."

She wanted a payout. Of course. Cash meant taxes. Worse, cash meant that if something happened to her the daughter-in-law and son-in-law were in control of a big chunk of money. She wanted a payout. This was exactly what I had expected and hoped for. Security Industrial didn't have the cash to match the bids I knew our competitors could make, but we could top their bids with a payout offer. A payout would let us make a higher bid. I offered her sixty payments over five years. I think she'd been hoping for this. She accepted our offer because it exceeded both of those tendered by the New Orleans companies. Again, we'd pay the notes from premiums that we would immediately start collecting.

Growth, without cash, without increased expenses. Again, the cream paid for the cow.

The MBA students from LSU come to my house in New Orleans to ask which acquisitions were the most important, which ones turned the game in our favor. They're looking for the big plays, the eighty-yard runs that gave us the championship. All I can tell them is we put our blood and sweat into each one; they were all important. When you're in the heat of the battle, the game rides on the one you're working on right then. I can remember every one.

"Old Lucky," the worn and tattered brown leather briefcase I took to all fifty-six acquisitions, bears the battle scars. Deep scratches from table corners, a stain or two from spilled coffee, zipper torn past functioning. Our people in Donaldsonville urged me to replace Old Lucky, but I wouldn't do it. She'd carried me through too many hard times, been by my side in too many battles, stayed with me win or lose. When we sold the business, they put Old Lucky in a frame and hung her on the wall, like a trophy. But I think of her as a comrade in battle.

I kept a blackboard in my office in Donaldsonville, on which someone would write, "Congratulations on acquisition number 10" (or 16, or whatever had been our most recent one). Below that it said, "Go for number 11." The Poole place was number 12.

For me, the next one was always the most important, the one I had to win. We were always working on one. If we didn't have one in our sights, I got restless. I might say to Sidney Harp or Jesse Arboneaux, "Come on, let's take a ride." I'd grab Old Lucky and we'd just go out and drive through the small towns until we found a funeral home that looked like a prospect. I'd think, *Maybe this will be number 13 or 14.* We'd go up and knock on the door and ask for the owner, just as we did with Geesey-Ferguson.

"I'd be interested in buying your funeral home."

I'd say it flat out. Why beat around the bush? Sometimes, as with Geesey-Ferguson, they'd just tell me to clear out. But I'd come back, and eventually we might do business. I had an itch to grow, to do a little better than I was doing.

But the bigger we got with Security Industrial companies in towns like Amite, Hammond, New Iberia, Baton Rouge, Alexandria, Shreveport, Ruston, Lafayette, and Monroe, the clearer it became that to win the state championship we had to have a presence in New Orleans. I guess you could say New Orleans was our Bastogne.

The color of money

In 1965, after nearly twenty acquisitions around the state, we got a toehold in New Orleans with the acquisition of Community Funeral Insurance Service and American Hemlock Insurance. Then, in 1971, we acquired a bigger outfit: Standard Life Insurance Company of New Orleans.

That was number 31, and a big one, not only because it was in New Orleans but also because it was the largest black-owned insurance company headquartered in the state. Dr. Clarence Haydel owned the controlling interest in Standard Life. His son-in-law, Dutch Morial, who became a prominent and highly regarded New Orleans politician, was at that time Louisiana's first black state legislator. He sat on the first row but was not well treated by his colleagues in the legislature and was generally snubbed by businesspeople who regularly courted favor with legislators. No one took Dutch out to dinner. Except me. I couldn't afford big, expensive steak dinners, so we went where they served chili or hot dogs. After a while we became friends. We'd both had our share of being treated as interlopers.

When I learned that Standard Life was accepting bids, I asked Dutch to put in a word for me with his father-in-law, Dr. Haydel. He agreed to do so, but he cautioned me that his father-in-law never listened to his advice. The three of us met to discuss my bid of $3.5 million. Dr. Haydel, who seemed to have misgivings, asked Dutch what he thought. Dutch took a long time before replying. He rubbed his chin till I feared he would rub the skin off. Finally, he spoke up:

"You know, you're always worrying about race. But I think we should be concerned about other things."

"What do you mean?" Dr. Haydel asked.

"Not about race," Dutch said.

I supposed he was about to tell his father-in-law that it was perfectly acceptable to do business with a white man. I knew we were bidding against a large black-owned insurance company based in Atlanta, Georgia. Dr. Haydel worried about his company remaining a black company. If he sold to us, rather than to the Atlanta outfit, a black company might become a white company. He felt this was somehow disloyal. Was he selling out his heritage?

But this wasn't the issue his son-in-law had in mind.

"It's not about race, or heritage, or tradition, not about black and white," Dutch went on, slowly, thoughtfully stroking his chin. "But it is about color, the color – green, the color of money. In business you accept the best deal. That's it."

He pointed out that we had submitted the best bid, offered the most money.

"Mr. Ourso's bid is $1 million better than the competition's," he observed.

Dutch told Dr. Haydel that in business the important color is green, that black and white are irrelevant.

This acquisition of an important New Orleans company took place about the time I joined the Young Presidents Organization.

In 1973 and 1974 we added two more New Orleans businesses: Good Citizens Life Insurance Company and Ranson Industrial Life Insurance Company. The Ranson place was run down. It didn't look like much, but we renovated it, gave it some class and dignity.

So, by the mid-1970s we'd established a beachhead in New Orleans. Nevertheless, the big boys still considered us interlopers. Not a New Orleans outfit. Not one of them. We got the feeling we were not welcome.

The 1980s were our biggest years for acquisitions, especially in New Orleans. We called them our "go-go years." Seventeen acquisitions in all, thirteen of them in New Orleans.

In 1981 we submitted sealed bids to the Lamana, Pano, and Fallo families for Atlas Life Insurance Co. and a funeral home company, both owned by these families. Though we won in our bid for Atlas Life, we were told ours was not the winning bid for the funeral homes, which went to the Tharp-Sontheimer Group, a big New Orleans outfit. As it turned out, it didn't matter that we lost in our bid to acquire this business. For the following year we picked up the Lamana-Pano-Fallo companies when we acquired Delta Life Insurance and Funeral Company and Tharp-Sontheimer, both owned by a single family.

Tharp-Sontheimer had six places. In 1982 I negotiated with their president, Leonard Wolfe, as well as their stockholders, every day for a week. Finally, one morning Leonard called to tell me the family had held a meeting the evening before and had come to an agreement. They could accept $20 million, for sure. Nineteen, maybe. I was sweating because I knew we couldn't pay nineteen. We ended up getting it for $18.5.

Also in 1982 we acquired the Orleans Insurance Company, and then the home service division of Riverside Life Insurance Company in 1983.

With the purchase of Tharp-Sontheimer, we circumvented efforts to keep us out of the city. In my mind, the Delta Life and Tharp-Sontheimer acquisitions were a turning point for us. After that we weren't the little guys from Donaldsonville. When we were closing for Tharp-Sontheimer, Leonard Wolfe took me aside.

"You're the big guy now," he told me.

I wasn't sure what he was talking about. He explained that with the purchase of Tharp-Sontheimer, we had acquired eight shares in "the Shed," the New Orleans Limousine Company, which provided the limousines for most of the funeral homes in the city. So with the five shares we had from earlier acquisitions, we now had thirteen shares. How did that make us the big guys? Well, there were only twenty shares outstanding. We held a controlling interest. If you controlled the Shed, you were the big guy. That's the way Leonard Wolfe saw it.

The Battle for New Orleans

As I've said before, in nearly half a century we acquired fifty-six companies or parts of companies. We acquired the first twenty-five with no money, no cash. If you can develop the existing intellectual assets of the acquired company – that is, if you can motivate the people – you can pay the notes with premiums. So when I went to Harvard with the Young Presidents Organization and told fellow members about how we sold burial insurance in Donaldsonville, I quickly got the nickname "No-cash Ourso." However, after a while, we had the option of acquiring companies for cash, which for some owners was more attractive than a payout. The cash option broadened our field of opportunity and helped us to establish Security Industrial in New Orleans.

The seven families involved with Jacob Schoen and Son, Inc. of New Orleans wanted cash. We bid $8.3 million, which I thought was a decent and fair offer.

The acquisition of Jacob Schoen, a large and old New Orleans establishment, in 1986 was our Bastogne in the Battle of the Bulge. This acquisition could fairly be called "The Battle for New Orleans."

They had four funeral homes, including the main location on Canal Street and a place on Elysian Fields. The Canal Street home conducted more funerals than any other home in the state. I didn't think the New Orleans crowd would look at us as outsiders after we acquired this group of funeral homes. And if they did, it wouldn't much matter.

The night before the stockholder meeting the family's attorney, Philip Brooks, called to ask if we'd go up $100,000 on our $8.3 million bid. You see, since there were seven families involved in ownership of the company, they wanted a number that could be divided evenly by seven. I should have known. When you're dealing in cash, make your offer evenly divisible by the number of owners with whom you're dealing. Simple, but not something found in "the book."

"Okay, if we go up the $100,000, do we have a deal?" I asked.

"You have a deal," he assured me.

We went up $100,000.

As it turned out, the Schoen acquisition was more fraught with anguish and strife than I could have imagined. The difficulty surfaced when Margy and I met with the stockholders at the Elysian Fields home to formally present our offer. We all sat in the home's funeral parlor, the company's seven directors on a dais in front, the sixty stockholders, who represented the seven owning families, in the seats usually occupied by mourners. I presented our bid to the stockholders and took my seat beside the directors.

I set Old Lucky on the floor at my side, battered and ragged, worn and torn. No matter. Old Lucky had carried me this far; I wasn't about to trade her in.

I knew we had a deal. I was confident, but my heart was racing.

At the meeting's commencement, Margy and I had distributed to the stockholders strawberries, pecans, shrimp, and crawfish bisque which we'd packaged and frozen. I believed we would win, and was pleased to be able to share good things from Donaldsonville with these people from New Orleans.

Let me tell you, Margy and I had been hard at work the previous day, preparing the containers of crawfish bisque. Whew, what a ton of work! You hollow out the "heads" and grind up the tail meat with spices and then stuff the "heads" before putting them into the bisque. Crawfish bisque is not easy to come by; it's a rare gift. But we wanted these city folks to know that country people were generous, sharing people.

In my mind, I could see acquisition number 46 being erased and number 47 being written on my blackboard back in Donaldsonville.

Bobby Schoen, president of Schoen & Son, took the podium. All that remained was the directors' vote. I tasted the victory.

This taste turned sour. A Schoen employee came quietly from the back of the funeral home into the parlor and stepped up on the dais to hand Bobby Schoen a note and an envelope. He stepped away from the microphone to read what was written on the note, then in a whisper he conferred with the directors who sat behind him. I couldn't hear what they were saying.

I soon learned what transpired. Frank Stewart, a competing bidder for the funeral homes and owner of the Lake Lawn Metairie Cemetery, knew of the impending meeting and had dispatched his lawyers and accountants to our meeting. His emissaries were in an office in the building's rear, and now, at the meeting's critical moment, he was trying to submit a bid that would top the one I had made.

The bid I had just presented was $8.4 million. I had understood us to have a deal. But two of the five directors served also on the Lake Lawn board and, as the meeting progressed, I sensed that they were not in favor of approving my bid.

What a complicated and tangled web. Why would you find two Schoen directors serving on the board of a competing funeral home? Well, because Schoen owned a 49% voting right in a joint venture with Frank Stewart and Lake Lawn. On land owned by Lake Lawn, Schoen and Stewart had recently built a funeral home. The ownership was fifty-fifty, but since Stewart had put up the land, voting rights were divided so as to give Stewart 51% and Schoen 49%.

To further complicate matters, there was in place an agreement which stipulated that if one party were to get out of the joint venture for any reason, he would have to pay what amounted to a penalty – the amount to be determined by a formula which considered the last five years' profits or losses.

Stewart's people were obviously trying to block the acquisition, and failing that, they were demanding a $1 million penalty payment from Schoen – or its new owner – for withdrawing from the joint venture.

All of this came out in the debate which ensued. My spirits sank.

I gave Old Lucky a mournful glance. Lord help me. I hadn't been told about this agreement, hadn't known about the two directors on both boards. Moreover, it appeared that Stewart's eleventh-hour offer was causing the board to hesitate on giving final approval to my offer.

And, as the two Lake Lawn directors pointed out, Stewart was, after all, one of them, a New Orleans boy. E.J. Ourso was "not one of us." Not one of them. No, he's from Donaldsonville. Stewart's people made us out as interlopers, outsiders. Our deal seemed to be collapsing in the heat of the debate.

Talk about getting knocked down. I had brought them good things to eat from Donaldsonville, as if to say we're generous and sharing people. I placed on the table a very generous offer besides. I easily agreed to raise my original offer by $100,000 to accommodate the seven families. A number evenly divisible by seven had cost us an extra $100,000. We weren't hard to get along with. Friendly country people. We had trusted we had a deal.

Oh, but Stewart had been angling for Schoen for years, making offers that were well below the one we had made. But now here Stewart was, his prize about to slip away, with a last-ditch effort to stop us from acquiring Schoen and Son.

I had believed Schoen to be a company that played by the rules. That was their reputation. The taste in my mouth wasn't of victory but canvas and blood. I'd been knocked down.

I got up.

A tear of frustration slid down my cheek. I picked up Old Lucky. Bobby Schoen stood aside to let me have my say. The sixty stockholders fell silent. I turned to the directors behind me, so as to include them in what I had to say.

"Schoen is an old and respected New Orleans company," I began. "You've been in business for more than one hundred years – a century. That's a long, long time, more than one man's lifetime."

Bobby Schoen knew I was thinking about his grandfather, who had founded the firm, and about his father, both men of character and integrity. I went on:

"And in all that time Schoen has built and maintained a reputation for trust and fairness. Schoen is known as a firm of character. I thought we had a deal. I trusted the word of Schoen's attorney. So I am deeply saddened by what I have seen transpire here today."

Bobby nodded as if in agreement. I shook my head and sat down. What more was there to say?

It appeared there would be no number 47 on my blackboard tomorrow. I had had my say. But I felt deeply wounded, somehow touched at the core of life, where we are most vulnerable. Simply put, I felt betrayed.

A glimmer of hope returned when Bobby Schoen called for an executive session of the board, and the seven of them went into another room of the funeral home so they could speak freely and privately.

Margy and I stepped outside, out of sight of the shareholders who sat virtually silent in their chairs. I was unhappy and upset, and everyone knew it.

Security Industrial Insurance
Bases of Operation

The company had operations statewide, in each of the Louisiana towns and cities shown here. These included insurance offices, funeral homes and related businesses. Donaldsonville was headquarters for the entire time the Ourso family owned the company – 48 years, from 1948 until 1996.

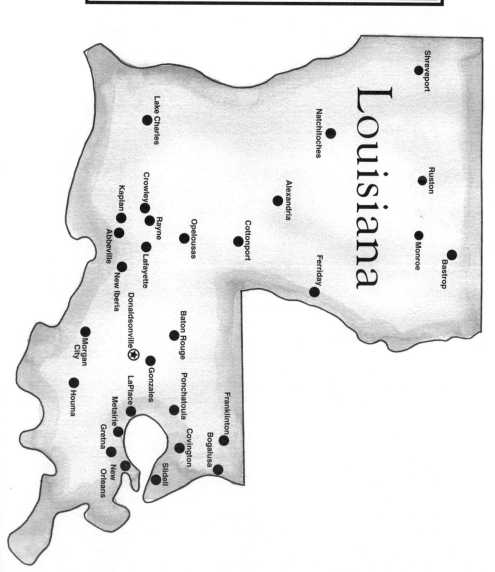

Louisiana

Shreveport
Natchitoches
Ruston
Monroe
Bastrop
Lake Charles
Alexandria
Crowley
Cottonport
Ferriday
Kaplan
Rayne
Opelousas
Abbeville
Lafayette
New Iberia
Baton Rouge
Donaldsonville
Morgan City
Gonzales
LaPlace
Ponchatoula
Franklinton
Houma
Metairie
Covington
Bogalusa
Gretna
Slidell
New Orleans

Margy put her hand on my shoulder, as she had so many times in the middle of the night when I lay awake worried about one thing or another.

"Don't get down in the mouth, Ous," she said. "It's alright; they didn't treat you fairly, that's all. It's not the first time, and it won't be the last."

Well, I was damned disappointed. I thought we had a deal. The man had said, "We have a deal." And I had taken him at his word.

We were still outside, after half an hour, when Philip Brooks came to meet us.

"Mr. Ourso."

"Yes, Philip."

"The company's yours."

"What?"

"You and I made a deal prior to this meeting, and the Schoen family will honor their commitment. You just bought yourself a funeral home company. Congratulations!"

"I did?" I said, then I let out a yell.

Margy was beaming.

"Now, let's go back inside and close this deal," he said, smiling.

And so we did. We signed the papers purchasing Jacob Schoen and Son for $8.4 million, as originally agreed.

It seemed that the sealed bid which Stewart had sent up to the front of the room was never opened. It was a matter of honor to the Schoen family: They had agreed to sell to us; they had given their word, so that was the end of it, as far as they were concerned.

This outcome infuriated Stewart. He demanded a $1 million penalty from us for Schoen's withdrawal from their joint venture – since we now owned Schoen and Son. The formula in their agreement assumed a funeral home could take ten years to become profitable. Then the most recent five years' profits were to be taken into consideration. Of these five, the highest and lowest years were thrown out and the amount was determined by the average profit of the three remaining years. Stewart's people set the figure at $1 million. One million dollars? No. The three years in question actually showed a loss, and Stewart's accountant used the absolute value of the loss, disregarding the minus sign! By this method, the greater the loss the higher the value of the joint venture. Stewart's interpretation of the formula was farfetched.

Stewart sued. He sued us every which way and any way he could, so determined was he to drive us from New Orleans. He sued us in the Orleans Parish Court for the $1 million he claimed was due him on the joint venture debacle. In Federal Court, he sued us under the antitrust laws, charging that with the purchase of Schoen, Security Industrial became a monopoly because it held a 70% share of the white funeral business in the parish. We argued that if all the funeral business in the parish were considered, black as well as white, our market share was only 50%. At the federal level markets were not segregated into black and white.

The newspapers played up the story, featuring profiles of myself and Frank Stewart, in which Stewart was cast as Old New Orleans and I as the newcomer.

After much legal wrangling, Stewart finally agreed to arbitration.

The arbitrator, as we expected, ruled in our favor, but not without much haggling and negotiating back and forth. He denied Stewart's arguments that with the purchase of Schoen we exercised monopoly power in the Orleans Parish market. He agreed that Stewart was entitled to the other 49% of the joint venture but disagreed with Stewart's interpretation of its value. The jointly owned home had on average operated at a loss. We were simply to let him have it. We would never have been any good as partners anyway after all the conflict and rancor between us.

So the acquisition of Schoen and Son stood.

Not long after, we acquired the remaining interest in McMahon-Coburn-Briede and full ownership of Bultman Mortuary Service, both of New Orleans, numbers 53 and 54. We'd already owned 50% of McMahon-Coburn-Briede. With this purchase, I went to each stockholder to get support for our offer. When we all got together in the same room, many of the stockholders wanted to sell. The acquisition took place in stages. But that was okay with us.

With controlling interest in the Shed and nineteen companies in New Orleans under Security Industrial's umbrella, we had done the unexpected. The home crowd was shocked. We had taken them by surprise. They hadn't figured that this country boy from Donaldsonville would be able to muster the resources to make such an assault on their bastion of old New Orleans establishments.

For nearly five decades I poured my blood, sweat and tears into building Security Industrial. Remember, you have to not only build the company, you have to maintain it day in and day out. This means attending to details day by day.

Somebody complains there's dust on chairs in a funeral home in New Orleans; someone else calls about holes in curtains in New Iberia. Imagine a funeral home, with all its parlors, furniture, accoutrements and so forth, and you have a list of what can and will go wrong and will need to be attended to in each home.

It can get you down, take your eye away from the big picture, the excitement of the acquisitions. But you better remind yourself that the details have to be seen to, or the big picture will disappear. Don't take the details for granted. I tended to the details for nearly fifty years – that's business day by day, seven days a week – no fishing, no hunting, no golf.

Still, the accumulation recorded in the numbers on my blackboard in Donaldsonville increased month by month, year by year. Our cash reserves built up and up, and the rising sales totals were published each month in *Security Progress*. All of this told us we were doing well. I led that old mule named "Progress" around and around the streets of Donaldsonville.

It was hard to believe we had started with assets of some $12,663 in 1948 and built up to assets in the hundreds of millions by 1990. Our reserves had risen from nothing to hundreds of millions; from the 1980s to the 1990s our profits had nearly tripled.

Oh, occasionally I'd get a taste of canvas and blood. Life never lets you wash away defeat completely. I guess that's a good thing; it keeps you from taking your station in life for granted.

CHAPTER 8

Dream Impossible
Dreams

E VERY SUCCESSFUL ENTREPRENEUR IS FIRST OF ALL
an impossible dreamer - a dreamer of impossible dreams. I, for
one, have done my share of dreaming. Like dreaming of marrying
a girl who's already engaged to be married, with all her sheets, towels
and pillowcases already embroidered with her fiancee's initials. Or dreaming of buying lawyer Lemann's grand house on Iberville Street, even
though I was waking up in the predawn dark wondering how I was
going to be able to make Friday's payroll.

If I'd told anybody about my dreams, they'd have locked me up.
Except Margy. Nothing I dreamed up surprised her.

What drove me to dream impossible dreams? My Donaldsonville
education? Five hungry children? Compound interest was one of my
main vehicles. But imagination, the dreaming of impossible dreams,
was my bridge to success. Imagination took me to where I am today.

What but imagination - thinking out of the box, impossible dreaming, call it what you like - tells you you can sell seven hundred chickens
in one summer? What but imagination tells you you can win the district basketball championship with six scrawny boys with weird nicknames from Donaldsonville? To get 200,000 soldiers from northern
France to Bastogne, Belgium, in the middle of winter in just forty-eight
hours took one hell of an imagination.

And another thing: If you don't think you can do it, if you don't
imagine that you can, then for sure you won't do it. But if you think

you can, then more than likely you will. Imagination, dreaming tells you you can. You see yourself succeeding. As the basketball floats off of your fingertips, you see it entering the hoop and hitting the bottom of the net. *Swish.*

But I must confess that at the start I had no idea where we'd end up. My dreams didn't reach very far out. How could I have thought that the little company Margy and I started with $10,000 would grow to be worth $180 million? The far future was foggy, blurry, ill-defined, to put it mildly.

But my imagination did work very intensely on what would happen tomorrow, or next week, or next month. It worked overtime on the near-at-hand. The avenues and streets of Donaldsonville, its houses and backyards, these things I saw vividly. I saw myself walking the streets I would walk, knocking on the doors I would approach. Immediate prospects preoccupied me. I imagined myself knocking on the back door of a certain family's house on a certain street, sitting at the kitchen table in dim, cold afternoon light on a January day, saying to the lady of the house, "It's not *if*, it's *when* you'll be the one who has to make funeral arrangements for your husband." I played over and over in my mind what I would say, how I would respond to what she said. I played out successful sales. I pictured in my mind what I would do tomorrow, or next week. How I would do a little better today, or this week, than I'd done yesterday, or last week. I played the scenes over and over, to be ready for all the turns the sales process can take.

Empathy, acting and role-playing: Creative tools of business

In business, imagination works on the details, little things to do to make a difference.

For example, my grandfather on my mother's side, Simon Falcon, a boilermaker, never had been in business. All his life he worked in a shop or factory. By the time my brother, Falcon, and I started out with the funeral home, Grandpa had retired. This left him with nothing much to occupy him, so he used to help us out at the funeral home. He'd come over to the home all gussied up in his best black suit and help us with the coffee room or other services we provided for the mourners. Caring for the bereaved kept him alive, among the living, where he preferred to be as long as possible.

Well, one day I was working the coffee room, helping the family of the deceased to coffee. Grandpa came up to me and beckoned me to follow him. We stood outside the room's doorway. He had a conspiratorial air about him.

"E.J.," he said, "I don't know a thing about business, but it seems to me that a tall, mannerly, well-dressed fellow like you could do a lot more good for himself if he were to be at the front door to greet people as they arrived. That's where you should be, E.J. Greet them when they come in. Shake hands with the gentlemen. Give the ladies a big hug and kiss - mind you, on the cheek, not on the lips."

He explained why he felt I should do this. He'd observed that most of the men who came had much younger wives. This was true, though I hadn't paid it much mind. He figured the chances were that the men would die first and the wives would be left to see to a proper funeral. If I would hug and kiss them, they'd be inclined to come to my funeral home when their husbands died.

Well, it may not sound like anything much, but this personal touch works. And Grandpa, even though he'd never been in business, could see what would make people want to come to our funeral home. He'd been to enough funerals to imagine clearly what might go through a mourner's mind, man or woman. When the ladies remembered how well they'd been treated, they'd want their visitors, when the time came, to get the same treatment they got at the Ourso home.

"Now if you were a new widow, wouldn't you go where you got such a nice welcome? That's where I'd go," Grandpa reasoned.

He saw the world the ladies saw. What did they fear? What concerned them? What would allay these fears and concerns? If Grandpa were a young lady, like those accompanying their older husbands to the funerals, this is what he would feel, this is what would bring him back when the time came.

That old boilermaker's imagination reported for active duty the day he retired. He didn't need rocket science to imagine how things might be. Ordinary life gave his imagination all it needed to get to work.

Grandpa taught me a lesson I should have remembered from Brother Hugh. He taught me again to put myself in the shoes of other people, to try to see things as other people saw them, to try to think their thoughts. If I was going to be in the business of taking care of other people's needs, then it behooved me to imagine the world as they saw it.

Brother Hugh had provided me with practice in this. All that memorizing and reciting of Shakespeare's lines, from Hamlet, or Macbeth, or Othello. To play the role of Hamlet, even for just a moment, for just a few lines, you had to put yourself in Hamlet's situation, see things as Hamlet saw them, think Hamlet's thoughts, and say what Hamlet said.

"If you want the audience to believe in Hamlet," Brother Hugh had said in so many words, "then you've got to express Hamlet's thoughts from Hamlet's point of view."

And in the process, of course, we learned a lot about what it was to be Hamlet. We acquired wisdom beyond our years and experience.

This applies directly to business, doesn't it? Every college of business ought to have a course about the function of dramatic imagination in business. Clear dramatic imagination could be applied to selling burial insurance and acquiring companies. At Security Industrial, we put it to work.

Before a big acquisition I'd round up my people – Jesse Arboneaux, John Fritz, Sidney Harp and, if it was in the summer, one or two of the interns like Mike Schott or Steve Hyde. We'd go in the back room of the office, and we'd act out the roles of the buyer (ourselves) and seller (say, Mrs. Poole, Leonard Wolfe, or the Schoens). We'd take turns being the bidder and seller. What objections would the seller raise? How would the bidder answer? And vice versa. We went over and over the Tharp-Sontheimer Group acquisition. I'd say, "I'm going to play Leonard Wolfe (president of the group); you be me and represent Security Industrial." And off we'd go.

"I'd like to buy the Tharp-Sontheimer Group," Jesse or Sid or John would begin.

"Not for sale," I'd say, speaking as Leonard Wolfe.

"Well, you might want to consider this," the bidder would say. "You know how it is with families. The original owners are getting along in years and now with the children coming up there are three or four families, not all of them directly or even indirectly involved in the business. I don't have to tell you the difficulties that makes for; it just keeps getting worse and worse the farther away from the founders you get. No offense, but isn't that how it's gone for a lot of companies? The children are less involved; they didn't go through the pain and trauma of building the business, so they don't have the same emotional investment in it."

And I'd respond, as Leonard:

"Who in the hell told you that?"

I might lean forward aggressively and pound on the table to emphasize my point.

"That's not a problem in our company, not in our family," I'd insist.

"Okay, but it's still a potential problem; it's not uncommon. So maybe you'd hear us out, hear what our offer is," Jesse would say.

This is the critical juncture, because once we make an offer, Leonard Wolfe, as president of the company, is obliged to bring it, no matter what it is, to the company's board. The right of refusal is theirs, not his alone. This is his fiduciary duty, even if he believes they'll reject it.

"Seventeen, seventeen million dollars. That's our offer," Jesse says.

"Not enough," Ourso/Wolfe replies. "We're talking about six companies, you know. Some of the stockholders might sell, but I can't see most of them going along with that."

Here Ourso/Wolfe pushes his chair back, as if to exit.

"So, what would it take?"

"Twenty-one, at least," I'd say as I rose to my feet.

"Twenty-one? Twenty-one? Come on. We can't go that high. But look, we'll guarantee jobs for the family members who want them. The children of the owners who want to be involved in the company can go on with it, and the others, well, they can cash in and be out of it.

Something for everybody," Jesse explains.

You can bet the question of what would become of family members who worked in the business is not far beneath the surface of Wolfe's mind.

"Nuts," Ourso/Wolfe says. "You guys are full of bull. I know you can come up with it. Why don't you go back to your office and go over the numbers?"

"Seventeen-five," Jesse says, upping the ante by half a million dollars. He knows the numbers; he knows our limits.

"They won't go for it. Get serious."

"Seventeen-five's our limit."

And so it would go, back and forth until we'd played it all out, raised all the objections we could think of, given all the replies we could think of, reversed roles, played the devil's advocate, rehearsed arguments and counter-arguments till we'd covered every objection we could imagine.

In real life, in the case of Tharp-Sontheimer, the question was how to negotiate the difference between our first offer of seventeen million and their asking price of twenty-one million dollars. Jesse knew there was no way we could do twenty-one, no way. If we'd come up, maybe they'd come down. Okay, let's try to imagine what might induce them to come down. And how could we come up?

Jesse, who worked closely with our finances, grew uneasy. He figured we might go seventeen-five. Where was the extra money to come from? How were we going to service all that debt?

As it turned out, after some side offers of employment for family members Wolfe took it to the shareholders. I think he urged acceptance of our bid. But he returned with a list of items they wanted to hold out of the homes: furniture, rugs, family heirlooms and antiques. The list got very long.

"Leonard, we would have to completely refurnish all the homes," I said.

We got the list whittled down to something we could live with, and they got the offer up to something they could live with. (They weren't quite ready to admit that, but we knew.)

"I've been told that this might work. Some want to sell for twenty, some will take nineteen. Eighteen is unlikely," Leonard informed us.

Jesse advised me that eighteen was about half a million beyond our limit. He was still uneasy. He'd done the numbers and didn't see us going over seventeen-five. I was ready to offer eighteen-five. It was an opportunity I didn't want us to miss. So after the last role-playing session, I called him back to try to get him to see the importance of this acquisition.

Oh, he knew it was important, knew that if we could pull it off we'd be the big dogs in New Orleans, knew how we'd been working toward that for years. But the numbers made him nervous. And he was right.

He was right on the money.

"Jesse," I said, "this is a big one, but worth it. Think of the synergies, the efficiencies we'll get. Are we going to get another opportunity like this? Sometimes you've got to play over your head. Is this the first time we've played over our heads?"

Jesse knew this one could do us in, but I wanted him to understand.

"When have we had a chance like this?" I asked him.

He finally was okay with it, he said, as long as I understood the downside risk.

Eighteen and a half million dollars, our biggest acquisition ever. It might have done us in, but it didn't. It was worth the eighteen and a half, and more. The company's intellectual assets – its people, their competencies, their experience – were strong and very valuable. The synergies and efficiencies were there. For example, we eliminated redundancies by locating functions, like embalming, in only one of the homes.

The role-playing we had done to prepare for this acquisition produced a benefit in addition to its value as a negotiating tool. As it freed the imaginations of our people, it let them out of the confining boxes of their company positions. When we played our roles, I was no longer president, managers were no longer managers, agents were no longer agents, arranged in the boxes of our organization chart. No, now we were all somehow liberated from those boxes and free to speak the mind, as we imagined it, of the person whose role we played. All the conventional lines of deference disappeared. In the back room, in the intense heat of the play, we each got outside of ourselves, so our role-playing carried benefits of personal growth too. We all delighted in it and relished it. It pushed us beyond the confines of our own narrow selves. We breathed fresher air. All of us were healthier for it. And so was our company.

On imagination, self-esteem and prosperity

As we went along, our dream horizons reached further out into the future. What had been obscure began to take on a shape. Small successes extended our imagination's reach, shedding light on the future, a little at a time. Without the day-to-day stuff, the smaller acquisitions, we might never have imagined the big ones.

The imagination's like a muscle: You've got to use it, stretch it out, get it in shape for the big events. Low self-esteem weakens the imagination till it won't reach out even for what's right in front of it. Low self-esteem wastes and diminishes the imagination; it causes the imagination to atrophy, like a muscle that becomes stiff, weak, unable to bend or stretch, and eventually useless. But high self-esteem strengthens the imagination, gives it reach, renders it flexible and supple.

"Dream impossible dreams," I tell the MBA students. "Think out of the box. Make up stories; then make them come true."

I explain to them that opportunity flows from the imagination. It's imagination that lets us bend our vision around corners and see clearly and vividly what's not normally within the eye's range. Without imagination you won't be inclined to try to look around corners.

I tell them entrepreneurs are compulsive people, compelled by their own imaginative natures to look around corners, to go for the extraordinary, to overperform, to surprise the hell out of everybody. Many people will tell you why you can't do something; you show them you can.

Oh, people out there will think you're crazy. That's why it's best to keep your plans to yourself. But don't forget: If you want to be an entrepreneur, dream big, impossible dreams. And then go out and make them real. Exercise a little imagination.

I imagined Security Industrial would become the largest industrial insurance company not only in New Orleans but in all of Louisiana. But if my associates and I hadn't dreamed it, would it have come to pass?

Out of the box and into the money

How entrepreneurs dream - that is, how they conceive of the business they're in - can have a powerful impact on their success.

Here's an example that has stayed in my mind many years. There was a fellow in the YPO who was with me at Harvard, a guy named Nicky Newman, whose father owned grocery stores in Omaha, Nebraska. On the first day of our seminar, the professor asked each of us what business we were in. When he asked Nicky, Nicky told him he was in the grocery business, the food business. The professor contradicted him:

"No, no that's not right. What business are you in?"

Nicky didn't know what to tell him. That night he called his father.

"Papa, what business are we in?" he asked.

"We're in the grocery business, the food business," his father answered.

"Well, that's what I thought, but our professor said, 'No, that's not right,'" Nicky reported.

"Come on home, son. I told you about those Harvard professors, trying to run down our success. Just get on a plane and come on home," Nicky's father told him.

But Nicky wanted to stick it out, so he stayed on, and each day when the seminar met, the professor began by asking Nicky what business he was in. And each day, upon Nicky's answering "the grocery business," the professor would say, "No, that's not it."

On the seminar's last day, the professor said to Nicky:

"The business you're in is the food distribution business."

"Oh," Nicky replied. He went back to Omaha with the notion that he wasn't in the grocery business but in food distribution. This was a whole new way of thinking about his business – and it changed everything for Nicky and his father.

When you think "grocery business," what do you imagine? Trucks coming in, trucks leaving, the grocery stores with shoppers, taking things from the shelves, lining up at the cash register? "Food distribution" opens up a whole new prospect. It's not *just* grocery stores; you can imagine grocery departments in big chain stores all over the country. You're thinking out of the grocery store box.

The following year at the YPO seminar Nicky sat in the first row, same professor. The professor asked him what business he was in.

"I'm in the food distribution business," he replied.

"Well, what big – excuse me, I mean little – differences has this made in your business," the professor inquired.

Poor Nicky, I was thinking, *Lord help him.*

"First, we went to J.C. Penny's and got them to lease us space for a grocery department in their Treasury stores," Nicky said. "Then we went to K-Mart and to Walgreen's Globe stores and to discount outfits all over the country and leased space for grocery departments there, too. Now we have grocery departments nationwide. We've started a whole new company to manage these grocery departments."

"So, how's business?" the professor wanted to know.

"Well, we haven't been in all of these stores for a full year," Nicky said. "But our revenues are over $100 million so far."

With that, all those who had been in the seminar the year before rose from their chairs and gave Nicky a standing ovation.

He made me think differently about my own business. This got me out of the box. I had been thinking of us as being in the burial insurance business. *No,* I thought, *that's not right.* Now, I began to think of us as being in the business of providing services and merchandise to bereaved families. So, we bought cemeteries in New Orleans and Baton Rouge; we got a flower shop and a limousine service, in addition to insurance companies and funeral homes.

It's all in how you imagine yourself. A narrow conception of your business is terribly limiting, exactly like being in a box. You've got to think out of the box. Don't let the way you have been thinking limit the way you can think. Dream your opportunities into being. With the professor's help, that's what Nicky did, and with Nicky's example that's what I did.

As for our professor, he had shown Nicky how to dream, how to think out of the box. I heard he went on to become a business advisor to General Motors. This was in the early '70s; General Motors was in need of some out-of-the-box thinking.

Napoleon Hill helps others to *Think and Grow Rich*

I've bought and given away thousands of copies of Napoleon Hill's *Think and Grow Rich*. I staple my business card to the inside of the front cover and write below it the date and "Compliments of E.J. Ourso" in green ink. I give Hill's book to anybody who will take it – to students, to employees, to people I meet at conferences, to people on Donaldsonville's streets.

When I talked to business classes at LSU, I took boxes of *Think and Grow Rich* and handed them out to whole classes, free. I try to make sure everybody I know has a copy.

In this book Hill reveals a fundamental principle of success: You greatly increase your chance of achieving success if you vividly imagine yourself achieving success – in whatever you set out to do. Make that image of success a fixture in your mind's eye. Sharply imagine what you want to achieve, and your chances of success improve. The image of vivid success constantly before you drives you to achieve it. You imagine you will overperform and so you do overperform.

What drives ordinary people to do extraordinary things? Imagination. That's why Hill told people they could think and grow rich. That's the "secret" message he broadcasts in every chapter, on every page.

I want everybody to grow rich, each in his or her own way. This is why I've given away so many copies of Hill's book.

Sometimes I feel like a preacher, delivering homilies. I've often said to students and others:

"Whatever you wish, whatever you dream, whatever you hope to achieve, whatever you try for, whatever you plan, it's yours, if you only believe."

Do you think I could have married Margy if I hadn't had her so vividly in my mind's eye – her green eyes, her smile, her face framed in wisps of brown hair – never mind that she was engaged to another man and that most of her aunts were against our marrying. If I hadn't believed, I'd have listened to Margy's cousin, Floyd Roberts, who told me to forget about Margy. With imagination and belief you can control your life to a great extent.

Imagination and belief are great motivators. When I say every successful entrepreneur is first of all an impossible dreamer, what I have in mind is not only that entrepreneurs possess the capacity to imagine things that do not exist in most people's plain sight but that entrepreneurs possess the capacity to convert other people into believers in their vision. Their vision is so strong, they believe in it so strongly, that they lead others to see it and believe it as well.

So when I talked to our agents, for example, about selling more insurance, I never talked to them about doing this for the company or simply to earn more money. I talked to them about the better car, or the better house in a better neighborhood, or the better schools for their children – all things they deserved for working harder and more effectively. I tried to put into their mind's eye the clear and vivid picture of the better life that they deserved. I helped them create a strong vision of the good life, told them I believed in them. I helped them dream big dreams, dreams they probably thought were impossible. To accomplish a dream, you've got to have the dream and believe in it. That's what Napoleon Hill says. And believe me, he's right.

Gen. Patton, 'The Jumping Padre' and the power of imagination

I've told you about General George Patton and the Battle of the Bulge and the siege of Bastogne. Patton had vision. He had worked out in detail how he would achieve his objective: the rescue of the 101st Airborne Division from the stranglehold of Hitler's army. He had worked it out in detail three times, in three different versions. Never mind the darkness and snow and sleet and ice.

The paths to success, in Patton's vision, were as clear as day. If they hadn't been, we never would have gotten there. For Patton, imagination was the bridge from where he was to where he wanted to be.

One of Eisenhower's generals expressed his lack of belief in Patton's vision:

"Wait a minute, George, you think you can do that, you think you can save those paratroopers? Remember, it's going to be snowing and sleeting and the roads are going to be bad."

He pointed out there'd be no air power to help our soldiers because of the weather. Now, do you think that a man with so depleted a vision as this general could have led our troops to victory?

Patton affirmed that he could get there:

"I'll get there, because if I can't, you'll just laugh at me."

And we mounted up – 200,000 men on trucks and tanks – and we hit the road like lightning cutting through the darkness and got there in forty-eight hours, just as Patton had promised Eisenhower and the generals.

When we got there, boy, my big guns, the 155 millimeters, began to thunder and kept on shooting three days and three nights straight. *Boom. Boom. Boom.* Without stopping. Even in that cold they got so hot I feared they were going to melt.

But we broke through the ring around Bastogne. Patton had imagined into being one of the most difficult, and crucial, of successes in the war.

It was on the day after Christmas that we broke through Hitler's ring around Bastogne and rescued the 101st Airborne Division. As our soldiers began to bring out the first of the men who had been besieged, there was this Army chaplain who came to me where we were, back from the lines, in the field firing our big guns.

"Lieutenant," he said to me, "do you think you can get me some people? I'm going to stand up on the hood of that jeep over there and say a Mass. So, please pass the word."

That chaplain – the man who looked through all the whirling chaos that surrounded us to see a clear picture of the beauty and meaning and healing power of the Catholic Mass – was Father Philip Hannan. We called him "The Jumping Padre" due to his association with the 82nd Airborne's paratroopers.

I did pass the word as he had requested, and within minutes some seven hundred soldiers had gathered around the jeep. Would you have thought a Mass would draw that many that fast in that place, in the ice and snow and cold? Not just Catholics, but Jews, Baptists and Presbyterians all gathered together there in the snow and ice on the hillside, under the cold, smoke-blackened sky.

The Padre got up on the jeep's hood, his thin figure silhouetted against the afternoon's waning light. Out of habit I took off my helmet, as did many of those who stood around me. Oh, it was cold. Padre Hannan put up his hand and began to speak.

"The first thing I want to tell you is keep your helmets on. Don't take off your helmets, as is your custom at Mass. Because I don't want to be writing a letter to your mother or wife or children, saying you survived the Battle of the Bulge but died of pneumonia caught at Mass the day after Christmas. I think the Good Lord will forgive us on this occasion if we stand and don't take off our helmets at Mass."

So we put our helmets back on. The Padre continued:

"If General Patton comes here – you know how he's always shouting to spread out, spread out, so one shell doesn't get us all – if General Patton comes here, it's every man for himself!"

There was laughter and applause.

"The Jumping Padre" conducted the Mass and gave Communion. I couldn't believe it. Everybody on the hillside took Communion. Before Communion he gave us a homily.

"You know, I may lose my commission, standing here in the cold, giving a homily, in the snow and the ice. I could lose my commission as a chaplain for having a homily, because I should let you get out of the weather and the cold. But it's the day after Christmas. And for three days before Christmas, as I was sitting in my foxhole or wherever I happened to be eating my K-rations, I could smell the turkey and the roast beef and the stuffing cooking in the oven, and the pies, and the cookies for the children. So I was thinking about that as I was eating my K-rations. Now, all you boys out here from the North, from above the Mason-Dixon Line, I'm sure you could smell that, too, just as I did," said the Padre, a native of Washington D.C.

Many in the crowd nodded and smiled. Yes, if they hadn't smelled it before, they did smell it now that he put it before them.

"But all you boys from the South...," he burst out suddenly, so that some of us jumped in surprise. "All you boys who come from down yonder below the Mason-Dixon Line, I know what y'all been smelling. I know you all been smelling that pork roast with plenty of garlic. That's what you been smelling!"

Cheers and rebel yells went up from all around, mine with the rest.

What a homily "The Jumping Padre" gave us. He knew how to carry us home. Each of us, for just that one instant, went back to where we had come from, back to where we each wanted to be. (As for me, I was in Mother's kitchen with my brother and sister and Mother's younger brothers, Stuart and Andrew.) We were all children again, soldier-children, I guess you could say, safe in our homes, warm for the moment, despite the cold in our bones.

I'll never forget the Padre's homily as long as I live. He gave us a vision of Christmas at home; in that war-torn world, he gave us the most impossible of dreams.

But his giving Communion to everyone puzzled me. I had thought Communion could only properly be given to Catholics, and only to Catholics who had been to confession. But everyone had taken Communion and there had been no confessions. So after the services were completed I went back to where the Padre was standing by his jeep.

"Padre, I don't understand. Tell me. All these men, you got Protestants and Baptists and Jewish people, not just Catholics. How can you give them all Communion? They didn't go to confession. So how can you give them Communion?" I asked.

I worried that what he had done was somehow sacrilegious, more harmful than beneficial. My strict Catholic upbringing had instilled in me the sacredness of the sacraments, which the Padre seemed to have disregarded.

"Lieutenant, when they commissioned me chaplain, they made me chaplain for all the armed forces, not just for Catholics, but for Jewish soldiers and Protestants, too," he said. "I guess when the boys of these other faiths saw the Catholics receiving Communion, they wanted it, too. So, I just gave it to everyone. I didn't ask them if they were Catholic; I just gave it to them because they wanted it. That was enough for me."

He paused for a moment, smiling, untroubled by my question. He showed no fear of being burned at the stake. He continued:

"Now, when you came to take Communion, did I ask to see your Baptismal Certificate? Did I ask if you were a Catholic?"

"No."

"Well," he said, "I didn't ask them either. I just gave Communion to those who wanted it."

That day after Christmas was the most unforgettable day. During the Padre's Mass, they were bringing out the soldiers, the paratroopers of the 101st Airborne Division, who had been surrounded and pounded by Hitler's artillery for nearly two weeks, without proper food or medical supplies. They carried out guys on stretchers, some missing an arm, some without a leg, some without either leg, just stumps with bloody bandages. One after another, sorely wounded, on the stretchers they came out, headed away from the battle lines. Seemingly all of these wounded – as their stretchers approached the place on the hillside where they could see the men gathered for Mass – were drawn to the Padre's voice.

"Put me down, put me down. I want to participate in this Mass," many of them said, in so many words.

It was simply unforgettable. Unforgettable.

After the Mass the Padre went to every man where he lay on his stretcher and gave him Communion. He didn't ask whether they were Catholic. He gave to everybody who wanted it, regardless of religion. I can still see him going from stretcher to stretcher, among the blanketed, broken men, lying on the packed snow, the bloody bandages, the stumps, giving Communion to Catholic, Jew and Protestant alike. These were men who longed to commune with – and to thank – the benevolent God who had seen fit to bring them out alive.

I can still see the Padre's extreme care, answering a calling far above and beyond the commission of an Army chaplain, for each human being. One man's extreme care for other human beings in their extreme suffering. It's been six decades, but I see it clearly every time I think about it. It still brings tears to my eyes as it did on that day.

To my way of thinking, the Padre was and is a great man. That day after Christmas he did an extraordinary thing. His greatness lay in his imagination, in his capacity to imagine a better place for us – so that we could see it right then and there – a far better place than this world of darkness and impending doom.

Had General Patton come and found us gathered in that field – officers, men and the Padre – all huddled together in the cold and snow, there would have been hell to pay. Because just a single shell could have wiped out most of us. But neither the general nor the shell found us, protected as we were by a Divine Providence that was far beyond our ability to comprehend.

Prerequisite To Success: You've Got To Believe

SUCCESSFUL ENTREPRENEURS BELIEVE IN THEIR OWN impossible dreams. Without belief, impossible dreams are merely dreams.

Thinking out of the box, working hard, never quitting, getting back up and fighting again – these are all necessary ingredients of success. But plenty of people meet these requirements and still don't make it in the gate.

What more is required?

You have to *believe*. You have to believe in yourself and in what you're about. There are days and weeks when this self-belief is a hard row to hoe. Where do you get the strength to persevere, to get back up and fight?

When the New Orleans funeral home crowd tells you, "No, you're not one of us," how do you pick yourself back up off the canvas? Without the sustaining power of belief in yourself and what you're doing, how could you possibly get back up and fight?

Without belief in himself and his plans could General Patton have gotten 200,000 men and the equipment, guns and tanks to Bastogne in time to save the 101st Airborne? Do you think you can convince others of something you don't believe yourself? Your voice has to carry conviction. If Patton didn't believe it, why would Eisenhower believe it?

Strong self-belief comes first; it's the driver, the mover. It keeps your eye on the target.

Russell Conwell was a believer. He believed the good life was near at hand, buried like diamonds in your own backyard. If you didn't think you could find it there, you weren't likely to find it anywhere else either. A man could travel all over the world and miss the diamonds buried on his own farm. For the believer, success is near at hand, available to those with the desire and imagination to seize it. But you have to seize it.

A.P. Giannini was another believer. He believed in the Italian vendors of vegetables to whom he loaned money following the great San Francisco earthquake. Nobody else came forward to help these merchants. His opportunity was right there in his own wrecked city, brought to light by the earthquake itself. He proved it for all of us: Provide a needed service and you will prosper.

Brother Hugh was a believer. He believed in the practical application of dramatic imagination, which he demonstrated to his students at every opportunity. He believed we could win a district championship, and we won it.

And don't forget H.P. Williams. An ordinary man, he believed he could accomplish the extraordinary as a salesman, and he did.

Fr. Philip Hannan, "The Jumping Padre" – who went on to become the Archbishop of the Archdiocese of New Orleans – what a believer he was and is, maybe the greatest of them all. In the midst of war's whirl of death and chaos, he restored our hope and strength by reminding us of our homes back in America and our home with God in heaven.

Margy was a strong believer. In the darkest night, she would say, "Ous, it's okay, we're going to make it. You can do it." Her conviction made a believer out of me. Hearing Margy say it made all the difference in the world. Lord knows, our success is built upon belief.

Pope John Paul II once made this statement:

"Faith and reason are like two wings on which the human spirit rises to the contemplation of truth; and God has placed in the human heart a desire to know the truth – in a word, to know himself – so that, by knowing and loving God, men and women may also come to the fullness of truth about themselves."

I take this to mean that human reason is necessary but alone is not enough to bring us to the truth about ourselves. The truth without belief – without faith – loses its force. And where do we get the requisite faith and reason? Who bestows this faith and reason on human beings? Well, let me put it this way: We don't come by it on our own.

So, to succeed you have to be a believer, which means you have to have some help from the Divine. Believing in the seemingly impossible is a tall order. It's not hard to believe in what's clearly possible. When you see something clearly, right in front of you, belief is easy. But what about those things that aren't right in front of your eyes, things around the corner, out of sight? The things you have to imagine?

It's hard to believe in what seems to be impossible. As human beings we're capable of imagining the impossible; the capacity to *believe* the impossible is a Divine gift.

The chances we get, the hand we are dealt, these count for nothing if we don't seize them. The difference between success and failure is less in the opportunity than in the acting upon it. But again, we need the Divine push.

Margy and I got a lot of help from above all the way along the line. Sure, we worked hard, long hours, seven days a week, what with the five then six children and the business to run. We didn't sit around and wait for our good fortune to find us. It was out there, waiting for us to find it. Like Conwell's diamonds, it was there but we had to go dig it up.

From the beginning we thanked the Lord for giving us *the capacity* to do such work. Perseverance takes grit, but who hands out the allotment of grit? It all begins, and ends, with the Giver of All Gifts, the Divine.

So no matter what you do, be mindful of the fact that you don't do it alone. It would be a mistake to think you go it alone. This doesn't mean you can't be proud of your accomplishments and admire others for theirs. We're proud we've done well, proud that we've done good, proud of what the people who worked with us at Security Industrial did. But, Lord, never let us forget to be grateful for *the capacity* to do well and to do good.

Suggested Readings...

Acres of Diamonds (Russell Conwell)

Think and Grow Rich (Napoleon Hill)

A.P. Giannini: Banker of America (Felice A. Bonadio)

How to Win Friends and Influence People (Dale Carnegie)

The Power of Positive Thinking (Norman Vincent Peale)

The Greatest Salesman in the World (Og Mandino)

Working Smart: How to Accomplish More in Half the Time (Michael LeBoeuf)

The 7 Habits of Highly Effective People (Stephen R. Covey)

Tough Times Never Last, But Tough People Do (Robert H. Schuller)

Grow Rich! With Peace of Mind (Napoleon Hill)

My Life in Advertising/Scientific Advertising (Claude Hopkins)

The Master Key to Riches (Napoleon Hill)

The Lazy Man's Way to Riches (Joe Karbo)

Breakthrough Advertising (Eugene Schwartz)

The Start-Up Entrepreneur (James R. Cook)

Confessions of an Advertising Man (David Ogilvy)

Ogilvy on Advertising (David Ogilvy)

Direct Mail and Mail Order Handbook (Dick Hodgson)

How to Make Money in Mail Order (Melvin Powers)

Secrets of a Successful Mail Order Guru: Chase Revel (Ron Tepper)

Successful Direct Marketing Methods (Bob Stone)

The Greatest Direct Mail Sales Letters of all Time (Dick Hodgson)

Tested Advertising Methods (John Caples)

How to Write Good Advertising (Vic Schwab)

The Robert Collier Letter Book (Robert Collier)

How to Write, Speak and Think More Effectively (Rudolf Flesch)

Writing That Works (Roman and Raphaelson)

Direct Mailing Success: What Works and Why (Freeman Gosden)

Maxi-Marketing (Rapp and Collins)

How to Get Ideas (Jack Foster)

Think Out of the Box (Mike Vance & Diane Deacon)

Invest First, Investigate Later (Robert Slater)

Sources

Ambrose, Stephen E. *Citizen Soldiers*. New York: Simon and Schuster [Touchstone edition], 1998.

Arboneaux, Jesse. Personal interviews. June 1999 – Feb. 2000.

Conwell, Russell H. *Acres of Diamonds*. New York: Berkeley Publishing Group [Jove edition], 1978.

Crifasi, Brother Eldon. Personal interview. July 15, 1999.

Deville, Karen. Personal interviews. June 1999 – Feb. 2000.

Esquivel, Dan. Personal interview. Oct. 1999.

Falcon, Stewart. Personal interview. Feb. 2000.

Folse, John. Personal interview. Feb. 12, 2000.

Harp, Sidney. Personal interview. Oct. 25, 1999.

Hill, Napoleon. *Think and Grow Rich*. New York: Ballantine Books, 1983.

LeBlanc, Cathy. Personal interviews. June 1999 – Feb. 2000.

Lovett, Janice. Interview with E.J. Ourso in Donaldsonville. Audiocassette. Sept. 8, 1996.

Marchand, Sidney A., Sr. *The Chief in the Land of the Chetimaches*. Donaldsonville, La.: Louis A. LeBlanc, 1959.

Nash, Gerald D. *A.P. Giannini and the Bank of America*. Norman, Okla.: University of Oklahoma Press, 1992.

Ourso, E.J. Speech. Videocassette. Aug. 1996.

——,Talk at LSU College of Business Administration Reception. Videocassette. Oct. 2, 1996.

——, Talks with LSU MBAs. Videocassettes. Oct. 4, 1996 – Oct. 18, 1996.

—— and Dan Marin. 21 interviews at St. Charles Avenue residence, New Orleans. June 1999 – February 2000.

Smith, Jeannie. Transcription of interviews with E.J. Ourso.

Truex, Lenard [Brother Alton]. Phone interview. July 27, 1999.

Index

About E.J. Ourso...

E.J. OURSO, who owned Security Industrial Insurance Co. for nearly half a century, is considered one of the most successful businesspeople in Louisiana history.

Born on June 16, 1923, he started his career in business at age 10, selling scrap paper and iron during the Depression. He graduated in 1940 as salutatorian at Catholic High of Donaldsonville and went on to major in journalism and English literature at Louisiana State University. After three and a half years at LSU he was called to active duty in the U.S. Army. He served in the European Theater and was an artillery officer at the Battle of the Bulge under Gen. George Patton.

Following the war he married Marjory Barbier, and they had six children. They started Security Industrial Insurance in 1948 with $10,000 capital and sold the company in 1996 in a deal valued at $180 million.

Philanthropists for most of their business careers, the Oursos provided support for unwed mothers with stillborn babies, the poor of their own community of Donaldsonville, and impoverished religious nuns, brothers and priests, among others.

He is a recipient of the St. Louis Medallion (given by the Catholic Archdiocese of New Orleans), was named a Knight of St. Gregory by Pope John Paul II, and received an honorary Doctorate of Humane Letters from LSU. In 1996 the LSU Business School was renamed for him; it became the E.J. Ourso College of Business Administration.

About Dan Marin...

DAN MARIN teaches business ethics and business strategy in the William W. and Catherine M. Rucks Department of Management at Louisiana State University in Baton Rouge. He came to LSU in 1984 to serve as Director of the Masters of Business Administration program. Later he was an Associate Dean of LSU's E.J. Ourso College of Business Administration, before joining the Management Department.

He holds a BA in English from Oberlin College in Ohio, a PhD in English from the University of Iowa, and an MBA from the University of South Carolina, where, for eight years, he taught in the Department of English. For four years he was training director for Columbia, S.C., newspapers.

He has published fiction, nonfiction, poetic translation, literary criticism, and scholarly articles about business theory and business communication. He and his wife, Ali, have reared three daughters. They live with their youngest in Baton Rouge.

Inspiring Books
from
ACADIAN HOUSE PUBLISHING

Dreaming Impossible Dreams
Reflections of an Entrepreneur

This 176-page autobiography is the rags-to-riches story of multimillionaire philanthropist E.J. Ourso of Donaldsonville, Louisiana, the man for whom the LSU Business School is named. It reveals how Ourso acquired 56 businesses in 48 years – the first 25 with no money down. A testament to the effectiveness of the American free enterprise system, the book chronicles Ourso's life beginning with his early years as a salesman. It reveals his secrets to the acquisition of wealth. (Author: E.J. Ourso with Dan Marin. Hardcover ISBN: 0-925417-42-4, Price $22.95; Softcover ISBN: 0-925417-43-2, Price $14.95)

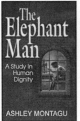

The Elephant Man
A Study in Human Dignity

The Elephant Man is a 138-page softcover book whose first edition inspired the movie and the Tony Award-winning play by the same name. This fascinating story, which has touched the hearts of readers throughout the world for over a century, is now complete with the publication of this, the Third Edition. Illustrated with photos and drawings of The Elephant Man. (Author: Ashley Montagu. ISBN: 0-925417-41-6. Price: $12.95.)

Why Men Watch Football

Why Men Watch Football is a 172-page hardcover book that is the definitive work on a subject that millions have asked themselves at one time or another: Why *do* men watch football so much? The book is a serious study of the male psyche, and it also has a humorous side. Illustrated with photos. (Author: Bob Andelman. ISBN: 0-925417-14-9. Price: $14.95.)

Water From Stones
An Inner Journey

Water From Stones is a 128-page hardcover book that is designed to serve as an instrument of healing, renewal and enlightenment for those who are seeking to walk a spiritual path. It is a book for those who are willing to take positive steps toward a more meaningful, more joyful life. The author maintains that the events and circum- stances that test our hearts and spirits can bring forth our greatest gifts. She points out that spiritual and psychological healing comes to us as we learn and accept what she refers to as "the lessons of the desert." (Author: Lyn Holley Doucet. ISBN: 0-925417-40-8. Price: $12.95.)

The Forgotten Hero of My Lai
The Hugh Thompson Story

A 248-page hardcover book that tells the story of the U.S. Army helicopter pilot who risked his life to rescue South Vietnamese civilians and to put a stop to the My Lai massacre during the Vietnam War in 1968. An inspiring story about the courage to do the right thing under extremely difficult circumstances, regardless of the consequences. Illustrated with maps and photos. (Author: Trent Angers. ISBN: 0-925417-33-5. Price: $22.95)

TO ORDER, list the books you wish to purchase along with the corresponding cost of each. Add $3 per book for shipping & handling. Louisiana residents add 7½% tax to the cost of the books. Mail your order and check or credit card authorization (VISA/MC/AmEx) to: Acadian House Publishing, Dept. B-34, Box 52247, Lafayette, LA 70505. Or call (800) 850-8851.